MEDITERRANEAN
COOKBOOK
FOR BEGINNERS

*150 Mouthwatering Recipes
You Cannot Live Without*

BRITNEY MONROE

from the Publisher. All additional right reserved.

The information in the following pages is broadly considered to be a truthful and accurate account of facts and as such any inattention, use or misuse of the information in question by the reader will render any resulting actions solely under their purview. There are no scenarios in which the publisher or the original author of this work can be in any fashion deemed liable for any hardship or damages that may befall them after undertaking information described herein.

Additionally, the information in the following pages is intended only for informational purposes and should thus be thought of as universal. As befitting its nature, it is presented without assurance regarding its prolonged validity or interim quality. Trademarks that are mentioned are done without written consent and can in no way be considered an endorsement from the trademark holder.

Table of Contents

PART I 10

Chapter 1: Identifying the Mediterranean Diet..................................11

Defining the Mediterranean Lifestyle 12

The Rules of the Mediterranean Diet.. 13

Chapter 2: Savory Mediterranean Meals 16

Mediterranean Feta Mac and Cheese 16

Chickpea Stew... 16

Savory Mediterranean Breakfast Muffins................................ 17

Mediterranean Breakfast Bake.. 18

Mediterranean Pastry Pinwheels 20

Chapter 3: Sweet Treats on the Mediterranean Diet.......................... 22

Greek Yogurt Parfait... 22

Overnight Oats 23

Apple Whipped Yogurt 24

Chapter 4: Gourmet Meals on the Mediterranean Diet........................ 25

Garlic-Roasted Salmon and Brussels Sprouts 25

Walnut Crusted Salmon with Rosemary................................. 26

Spaghetti and Clams 27

Braised Lamb and Fennel 28

Mediterranean Cod... 30

Baked Feta with Olive Tapenade.. 31

Chapter 5: 30-Minutes or Less Meals.. 33

Vegetarian Toss Together Mediterranean Pasta Salad 33

Vegetarian Aglio e Olio and Broccoli..34

Cilantro and Garlic Baked Salmon...35

Harissa Pasta...36

1 Hour Baked Cod...37

Grilled Chicken Mediterranean Salad..38

Lemon Herb Chicken and Potatoes One Pot Meal.................................40

Vegetarian Mediterranean Quiche..42

Herbed Lamb and Veggies...43

Chicken and Couscous Mediterranean Wraps..44

Sheet Pan Shrimp...46

Mediterranean Mahi Mahi..48

Chapter 7: Slow Cooker Meals..**50**

Slow Cooker Mediterranean Chicken...50

Slow Cooker Vegetarian Mediterranean Stew...52

Vegetarian Slow Cooker Quinoa..54

Slow-Cooked Chicken and Chickpea Soup...56

Slow Cooked Brisket...58

Vegan Bean Soup with Spinach..59

Moroccan Lentil Soup..60

Chapter 8: Vegetarian and Vegan Meals...**62**

Vegetarian Greek Stuffed Mushrooms...62

Vegetarian Cheesy Artichoke and Spinach Stuffed Squash....................63

Vegan Mediterranean Buddha Bowl..65

Vegan Mediterranean Pasta..67

Vegetarian Zucchini Lasagna Rolls..68

Vegetarian Breakfast Sandwich...69

Vegan Breakfast Toast..72

Vegetarian Shakshouka 73

PART II 75

Chapter 1: The Power of the Crock Pot and Its Benefits 76

Chapter 2: Healthy Breakfast Recipes 79

Boiled Eggs 79

One-Hour Bread 79

PART III 114

Chapter 1: Introduction to the Heart-Healthy Diet 115

The Rules of the Heart-Healthy Diet 115

The Benefits of the Heart-Healthy Diet 117

Chapter 2: Heart-Healthy Savory Meals 119

Shrimp Scampi and Zoodles 119

Citrus Chicken Salad 120

Shrimp Taco Salad 122

Chicken, Green Bean, Bacon Pasta 123

Heart-Healthy "Fried" Chicken 125

Turkey Burgers and Slaw 126

Slow Cooked Shrimp and Pasta 128

Chapter 3: Heart-Healthy Sweet Treats 129

Chocolate Mousse 129

Baked Pears 130

Chocolate Peanut Butter Bites 130

Oatmeal Cookies 131

Pina Colada Frozen Dessert 132

Kiwi Sorbet 132

Ricotta Brûlée 133

Chapter 4: Heart-Healthy Gourmet Meals 134

Grilled Halibut With Pine Nut Relish 134

Shrimp Bowls..135

Grilled Watermelon Steak Salad...136

Crispy Cod and Green Beans 137

Pistachio-Crusted Fish 138

Cumin-Spiced Lamb and Salad..139

Chapter 5: Heart-Healthy Quick 'n Easy Meals 140

Sugar Snap Pea and Radish Salad..140

Horseradish Salmon Cakes...142

Salmon, Green Beans, and Tomatoes.......................................143

Broccoli Pesto Fusilli 144

Strawberry Spinach Salad 145

One-Pot Shrimp and Spinach..146

Chapter 6: Heart-Healthy Vegetarian and Vegan Meals..................... 147

Vegetarian Butternut Squash Torte...147

Vegetarian Fried Rice..148

Vegan Butternut Squash Soup 149

Vegetarian Kale and Sweet Potato Frittata.................................151

Vegan Ginger Ramen...153

Vegan Glazed Tofu 154

Vegan Greek Tofu Breakfast Scramble 155

PART IV 156

What is Plant-Based Eating? How Does It Differ From Veganism? What are The Health Benefits of Eating Plant-Based Food? 157

Chapter Two: 160

Clinical Studies: Science-Backed Proof 160

Chapter Three:...164

Basic Four-Week Meal Plan...164

PART V 176

UNDERSTAND THE RESISTANCE 177

INSULIN RESISTANCE DIET 181

LONG-TERM MANAGEMENT.......................................185

DIET PLAN...189

RECIPES...192

PART I

Chapter 1: Identifying the Mediterranean Diet

We know that certain diets are associated with better health—this is a simple fact of life. We've seen that entire groups of people live longer based on where they live, and to some degree, a good deal of that has to come from somewhere—it has to come from something like diet or environment. In this case, the diet of the people living in the Mediterranean has been found to be incredibly healthy for people—it has been shown that people who are able to enjoy this diet, who are able to eat fresh food by the sea and enjoy the benefits that it has, are able to be far healthier than those who don't have it. That is great for them—but what is their secret?

It turns out, it's all in the lifestyle. The Mediterranean lifestyle, food, and all, is incredibly healthy for you. Studies have shown that people living in Mediterranean countries such as Greece and Italy have been found to have far less risk of death from coronary disease. Their secret is in the diet. Their diet has been shown to reduce the risk of cardiovascular disease, meaning that it is incredibly healthy, beneficial, and something that the vast majority of people in the world could definitely benefit from.

The Mediterranean diet is recommended by doctors and the World Health Organization as being not only healthy but also sustainable, meaning that it is something that is highly recommended, even by the experts. If you've found that you've struggled with weight loss, heart disease, managing your blood pressure, or anything similar to those problems, then the Mediterranean diet is for you.

When you follow this diet, you are able to bring health back to your life and enjoy the foods while doing so. It's perfect if you want to be able to enjoy your diet without having to worry about the impacts that it will have on you.

Defining the Mediterranean Lifestyle

The Mediterranean diet is quite simple. It involves eating traditional foods based on one's location. Typically, in the Mediterranean, that is a diet that is rich in veggies, fruits, whole grains, beans, and features olive oil as the fat of choice. Typically, it involves elements beyond just eating as well. While it is important to have healthy food, it is equally important to recognize that the diet encompasses the lifestyle as well. In particular, you can expect to see a few other rules come into play.

In particular, the Mediterranean diet is unique in the sense that it encourages a glass of red wine every now and then. In fact, the diet is associated with moderate drinking, enjoying red wine several times per week, always responsibly, and in contexts that will be beneficial to the drinker. If you want to be able to enjoy the Mediterranean diet and you are pregnant, or against drinking, you can do that, too—but traditionally, the red wine is included and even encouraged in moderation thanks to the antioxidants within it.

Additionally, on the Mediterranean diet, it is common to share meals with friends and family. This is essential—eating is more than just filling the body, it is nurturing the mind and relationships as well. This also comes with the added benefit of also being able to slow down eating—when you are eating the foods on this diet, you will discover that ultimately, you eat less when you're busy having a riveting conversation with someone. The fact that you are slowed down with your eating means that you will fill up sooner and realize that you didn't have to actually eat the food that you did. This means that you eat less and are, therefore managing your portions better as a result.

Finally, the Mediterranean diet focuses on physical activity. Traditionally, you would have had to go out to get the foods that you would eat each day, and that would mean that you'd need to get up, fish, garden, farm, or otherwise prepare your food. Eating locally is still a major component of this diet, as is getting up and being active. You need at least 30 minutes of activity, moderate or mild, per day. Even just walking for half an hour is better than nothing!

The Rules of the Mediterranean Diet

To eat the Mediterranean way, there are a few key factors that can guide you. If you know what you are doing, you can eat well without having to sacrifice flavor for health, and that matters immensely. When you look at the Mediterranean diet closely, you see that there are several tips that will help you to recognize what you need to do to stick to your diet.

Eating fruits and veggies

First, make sure that the bulk of your calories come from fruits and vegetables. You should be eating between 7 and 10 servings of fresh fruits and vegetables every single day—meaning that the bulk of your calories will come from there. Try to stick to locally grown foods that are fresh and in-season—they will have the highest nutritional value.

Reach for the whole grains

Yes, pasta is a major part of the diet in the Mediterranean, and you don't have to give that up entirely—but make sure that any grains that you are enjoying are whole-wheat. This allows you to enjoy foods that are high in fiber and are able to be digested differently than when you use refined carbs instead. While the refined carbs may give you instantaneous energy, they are also not nearly as good for you as whole wheat.

Using healthy fats

When it comes to flavoring or cooking your foods, you need to reach for the healthy fats first. This means choosing out foods that are cooked with olive oil instead of butter or dipping food in olive oil instead of butter. Olive oil, despite being a fat, has not been found to lead to weight gain when used in moderation. It is an incredibly healthy substitute for butter that is loaded up with all sorts of beneficial, heart-healthy antioxidants that will help your cardiovascular system.

Aim for seafood

When it comes to protein, fish, especially fresh fish, is the best choice. Fish should be consumed at least twice per week, and it should be fresh rather than frozen whenever possible. In particular, it is commonly recommended that you reach for salmon or trout, or other fatty fish because the omega-3 fatty acids within them are incredibly healthy for you, and they will serve you well. Even better, if you grill your fish, you have little cleanup.

Reduce red meat

In addition to adding more seafood to your diet, you need to cut out the red meat. The red meats in your diet are no good for you—they have been linked to inflammation that can make it harder for your cardiovascular system.

Enjoy dairy in moderation

When you are on this diet, dairy is not out of the picture entirely. While you should avoid butter, for the most part, it is a good idea for you to enjoy some low-fat Greek yogurt on occasion and add in some cheese to your diet. It is a good thing for you to enjoy these foods to ensure that you have plenty of calcium to keep your body strong.

Spices, not salt

Perhaps one of the most profound differences between most other diets and the Mediterranean diet is the lack of salt. The Mediterranean diet reaches for herbs and spices before adding in salt, meaning that you will be consuming less of it over time. Even better, you will grow to love your new foods without needing salt.

Chapter 2: Savory Mediterranean Meals

Mediterranean Feta Mac and Cheese

Ingredients

- Egg (1, beaten)
- Feta cheese (8 oz., crumbles)
- Macaroni (0.5 lb., whole-wheat)
- Olive oil (3 Tbsp.)
- Salt and pepper to taste
- Sour cream (8 oz.)

Instructions

1. Cook pasta to instructions to create al dente pasta. Drain and place pasta into baking dish. Toss in feta and oil and mix well.
2. Combine your egg and sour cream with salt and pepper. Then mix well and toss over macaroni. Combine and bake at 350F for 30 minutes.

Chickpea Stew

Ingredients

- Bay leaf (1)
- Dry chickpeas (1 c., soaked overnight and peeled)
- Garlic (1 clove, cut in half)
- Lemon to serve

- Olive oil (0.25 c.)
- Onion (1, diced)
- Salt and pepper to taste

Instructions

1. Cover chickpeas in pot with just enough water to cover them and wait to boil. Then rinse and set into clean pot. Toss in all other ingredients but the lemon with just enough water to cover nearly one inch above the beans. Simmer for 2-3 hours and serve with lemons.

Savory Mediterranean Breakfast Muffins

Ingredients

Dry ingredients

- Baking powder (1.5 tsp)
- Baking soda (o.5 tsp)
- Flour (2 c.)
- Salt (0.5 tsp)

Wet ingredients

- Egg (1 large)
- Garlic (1 clove, minced)
- Milk (1 c.)
- Sour cream (0.25 c.)
- Vegetable oil (0.25 c.)

Fillings

- Cheddar cheese (2 c., shredded)

- Feta (2.5 oz., crumbled)

- Green olives (diced, 0.5 c.)

- Green onions (0.5 c., chopped)

- Roasted red peppers (0.5 c., chopped)

- Sun dried tomatoes (diced, 0.5 c.)

Instructions

1. Combine dry ingredients in a bowl. Mix wet ingredients in separate bowl. Combine the two together and mix.

2. Toss in fillings in as few stirs as possible.

3. Place in greased or lined muffin pan, dividing to all 12 recesses.

4. Bake for 25 minutes until golden-brown and crusty at 350F.

5. Cool for 10 minutes and serve warm.

Mediterranean Breakfast Bake

Ingredients

- Artichoke hearts (14-oz. can, drained)

- Bread (6 slices whole-wheat, chopped)

- Eggs (8)

- Feta cheese (0.5 c.)

- Italian sausage (turkey or chicken—1 lb., casings removed)

- Milk (1 c.)

- Olive oil (2 Tbsp., divided)

- Onion (1, chopped)
- Spinach (5 oz.)
- Sun dried tomato (1 c., chopped)

Instructions

1. Warm 1 Tbsp. of your olive oil on moderately high heat. Cook sausage for 8 minutes until it has browned, breaking it up as it cooks. Place it in a dish when it is done.

2. Toss in additional oil, then cook onion until soft, roughly 5 minutes. Toss in spinach until wilting (1 minute).

3. Combine eggs and mix in milk, bread, tomatoes, cheese, artichokes, sausage, and finally, the spinach mix.

4. Place everything in a 2.5 quart baking dish. Let sit for an hour in fridge, or leave overnight.

5. Let casserole sit for 30 minutes after removing from fridge. Then, bake for 45 minutes at 350F until brown. Let rest 10 minutes, then serve.

Mediterranean Pastry Pinwheels

Ingredients

- Cream cheese (8-ounce package, softened)
- Pesto (0.25 c.)
- Provolone cheese (0.75 c.)
- Sun-dried tomatoes (0.5 c., chopped)
- Ripe olives (0.5 c., chopped)

Instructions

1. Unroll pastry and trim it up to create 10-inch square.

2. Mix together your cream cheese and pesto until well-combined. Then, mix in other ingredients until combined. Place mixture in even layer across pastry, up to 0.5-inch of edges. Roll and freeze for 30 minutes.

3. Cut whole roll into 16 pieces.

4. Bake at 400F until golden, roughly 15 minutes. Serve.

Chapter 3: Sweet Treats on the Mediterranean Diet

Greek Yogurt Parfait

Ingredients

- Almond butter (2 Tbsp.)
- Fresh fruit (1 Tbsp.)
- Greek Yogurt (1 c.)

Instructions

1. Mix together yogurt and 1 Tbsp. of almond butter and put in a bowl. Top with fruit.

2. Warm remaining butter in microwave for 10 minutes, then drizzle atop yogurt. Serve. You can add different toppings to change up the flavor as well.

Overnight Oats

Ingredients

- Chia seeds (1 Tbsp.)
- Greek yogurt (0.25 c.)
- Honey (1 Tbsp.)
- Milk of choice (0.5 c.)
- Old fashioned whole oats (0.5 c.)
- Vanilla extract (0.25 tsp)

Instructions

1. Mix all ingredients into a glass container and leave in fridge for at least 2 hours but preferably overnight. Serve with berries of choice or other desired toppings.

Apple Whipped Yogurt

Ingredients

- Greek yogurt (1 c.)
- Heavy cream (0.5 c.)
- Honey (1 Tbsp.)
- Unsalted butter (2 Tbsp.)
- Apples (2, cored and chopped into small bits)
- Sugar (2 Tbsp.)
- Cinnamon (1/8 tsp)
- Walnut halves (0.25 c., chopped)

Instructions

1. Using a hand mixer, mix together yogurt, honey, and honey until it creates peaks.
2. Heat up your butter in a skillet over a moderate temperature. Cook apples and 1 Tbsp. sugar in pan. Stir and cook for 6-8 minutes until soft. Then, top with the rest of sugar and cinnamon, stirring and cooking an additional 3 minutes. Take it off of the burner and let it rest for 5 minutes.
3. Serve with whipped yogurt in bowl topped with apple, then sprinkle on walnuts.

Chapter 4: Gourmet Meals on the Mediterranean Diet

Garlic-Roasted Salmon and Brussels Sprouts

Ingredients

- Brussels sprouts (6 c., trimmed and halved)
- Chardonnay (0.75 c.)
- Garlic cloves (14 large)
- Olive oil (0.25 c.)
- Oregano (2 Tbsp., fresh)
- Pepper (0.75 tsp)
- Salmon fillet (2 lbs., skin-off—cut in 6 pieces)
- Salt (1 tsp)
- Lemon wedges to serve

Instructions

1. Take two cloves of garlic and mince, combining them with oil, 1 Tbsp. of oregano, half of the salt and 1/3 of the pepper. Cut remaining cloves of garlic in halves and toss them with the sprouts. Take 3 Tbsp. of your garlic oil and toss it with the sprouts in roasting pan. Roast for 15 minutes at 450F.

2. Add wine to the remainder of the oil mixture. Then, remove it from the pan, stir veggies, and place salmon atop it all. Pour the wine mix atop it and season with remaining oregano and salt and pepper. Bake 5-10 minutes until salmon is done. Serve alongside the wedged lemon.

Walnut Crusted Salmon with Rosemary

Ingredients

- Dijon mustard (2 tsp)
- Garlic (1 clove, minced)
- Honey (0.5 tsp)
- Kosher salt (0.5 tsp)
- Lemon juice (1 tsp)
- Lemon zest (0.25 tsp.)
- Olive oil (1 tsp)
- Olive oil spray
- Panko (3 Tbsp.)
- Red pepper (0.25 tsp)
- Rosemary (1 tsp, chopped)

- Salmon (1 pound, skin removed)
- Walnuts (3 Tbsp., finely chopped)
- Parsley and lemon to garnish

Instructions

1. Mix together the mustard, lemon zest and juice, honey, salt and red pepper, and rosemary. In a separate dish, combine the panko with oil and walnuts.
2. Spread mustard across salmon and top with panko mixture. Spray fillets with cooking spray.
3. Cook until fish begins to flake at 425F, roughly 8-10 minutes. Serve with lemon and parsley.

Spaghetti and Clams

Ingredients

- Clams (6.5 lbs.)
- Olive oil (6 Tbsp.)
- White wine (0.5 c.)
- Garlic (3 cloves, sliced)
- Chiles (3, small and crumbled)
- Spaghetti (1 lb.)
- Parsley (3 Tbsp., chopped)
- Salt and pepper to personal preference

Instructions

1. Prepare clams, soaking in clean water and brushing to remove all sand.

2. Warm 2 Tbsp. of oil in large pot. Then, toss in 0.25 c. wine, 1 of the cloves of garlic, and 1 chile. Cook half of the plans at high heat with regular shaking until clams are opened. Remove opened clams and their juices to a larger bowl. Repeat process with second half of clams. Discard any that do not open.

3. Prepare pasta according to packaging to create al dente pasta. Reserve 1 c. pasta water.

4. Warm remainder of oil (2 Tbsp.) in pot over moderate heat, tossing in remainder of garlic and chile. Cook until fragrant, then place all clams and their juices into the pot, tossing to coat well. Then, toss in pasta, mixing well to combine. If necessary, add in cooking liquid. Serve and season with salt/pepper to personal preference with parsley atop.

Braised Lamb and Fennel

Ingredients

- Bay leaves (2)
- Chicken broth (3 c.)
- Cinnamon stick (1)
- Fennel (1 bulb, chopped)
- Garlic head (chopped in half)
- Lamb shoulder (3 lbs., cut into 8 pieces)
- Olive oil (2 Tbsp.)
- Onion (1, chopped
- Orange (1 with peel, cut into wedges)
- White wine (1 c.)
- Whole peeled tomatoes (14.5 oz. can)

Instructions

1. Dry lamb and season with salt and pepper to taste. Warm oil inside a Dutch oven, and sear lamb on all sides, roughly 6 minutes each side. Move lamb to plate.

2. Place fennel, garlic, and onion in the pot and cook, until browning, roughly 8 minutes. Mix in wine and boil, deglazing the pan. Reduce heat and simmer until it has reduced 50%.

3. Toss in orange, bay leaves, tomatoes, broth, and cinnamon, plus the lamb. Simmer, then cover pot and transfer to oven set to 325F. braise for 1.5-2 hours. Remove lamb and place on clean plate.

4. Strain liquid left in pot, then return it to the pot to boil until thick, roughly 30 minutes.

5. Return lamb to pot to warm. Serve.

Mediterranean Cod

Ingredients

- Black olives (0.66 c., sliced)
- Cod (4 fillets, skinless)
- Fennel seeds (1 tsp)
- Lemon (1, sliced)
- Lemon (juice of ½ lemon)
- Olive oil (6 Tbsp.)
- Onion (1, sliced)
- Parsley (1 Tbsp., chopped)
- Salt and pepper to personal preference
- Tomatoes (0.66 c., diced)

Instructions

1. Warm olive oil at a moderate temperature, sautéing the onion with a pinch of salt until translucent, roughly 10 minutes.
2. Mix in tomato and olives, tossing in the juice as well. Allow it to simmer gently for roughly 5 minutes. Toss in fennel seeds and set aside.
3. Warm the rest of the oil in another pan and fry up the cod for 10 minutes, flipping halfway through until done.
4. Toss tomato sauce over heat to warm, then mix together the parsley, and serve atop the cod with a lemon slice.

Baked Feta with Olive Tapenade

Ingredients

- Baked pita or crusty bread to serve
- Feta cheese (6 oz.)
- Garlic (2 cloves)
- Green olives (0.33 c., sliced)
- Harissa paste (3 Tbsp.)
- Olive oil (3 Tbsp.)
- Parsley (3 Tbsp., fresh chopped)
- Roasted red peppers (16-oz. jar, drained)
- Salt (0.75 tsp.)
- Tomato paste (2 Tbsp.)
- Walnuts (0.5 c., halved)

Instructions

1. In a blender, combine your peppers, 0.25 c. walnuts, harissa and tomato paste, garlic, and 0.5 tsp of your salt until mostly consistent. It doesn't have to be perfect, but should be well combined.
2. Take half of mixture into baking dish that has been sprayed with cooking spray. Top with half of your feta, then spoon the rest of the red pepper sauce atop it.
3. Top with the last of the feta and bake until bubbly, roughly 25 minutes. Broil for the last 2.
4. While that bakes, make your tapenade. This requires you to combine your remaining ingredients together.

5. Remove mixture from oven and top with tapenade. Serve immediately with crusty bread or pita chips.

Chapter 5: 30-Minutes or Less Meals

Vegetarian Toss Together Mediterranean Pasta Salad

Ingredients

- Artichoke hearts (12 oz. jar, drained)
- Balsamic vinegar (2 Tbsp.)
- Kalamata olives (12-ounce jar, drained and chopped)
- Olive oil (2 Tbsp.)
- Pasta (8 oz., wheat)
- Salt to personal preference
- Sun-dried tomatoes in oil (1.5 oz. jar, drained)

Instructions

1. Prepare pasta according to packaging.

2. Mix together olives, tomatoes, and artichoke.

3. Drain pasta and add them to a bowl with artichoke mixture. Then, top with vinegar and olive oil, mix well, and serve warm.

Vegetarian Aglio e Olio and Broccoli

Ingredients

- Olive oil (3 Tbsp.)
- Cayenne peppers (3)
- Garlic (3 cloves, sliced)
- Broccoli (1 head, prepared in florets)
- Spaghetti (7 oz. whole wheat)
- Salt to taste

Instructions

1. Boil water and prepare spaghetti according to instructions until al dente. Drain and reserve.

2. In a pan, heat up 1 Tbsp. of your olive oil at a moderate temperature, then toss in the garlic and peppers, sautéing until fragrant. Remove garlic from heat and set aside.

3. Toss broccoli into pan and cook for 4 minutes. Then toss in spaghetti, garlic, and remaining oil. Cook for an additional minute or two, then serve.

Cilantro and Garlic Baked Salmon

Ingredients

- Cilantro (stems trimmed)
- Garlic (4 cloves, chopped)
- Lime (0.5, cut into rounds)
- Lime juice (1 lime's worth)
- Olive oil (0.5 c.)
- Salmon fillet (2 pounds, skin removed)
- Salt to taste
- Tomato (cut into rounds)

Instructions

1. Allow salmon to come to room temp for 20 minutes while oven preheats to a temperature of 425 F.
2. While you wait, take a processor and combine garlic, cilantro, lime juice, and olive oil with a pinch of salt. Combine well.
3. Place fillet into baking pan that has been greased. Top with a light sprinkle of salt and pepper. Then spread cilantro sauce atop fillet, coating whole salmon. Top with tomato and lime.
4. Bake for 6 minutes per 0.5 inch of thickness (1-inch fillets take around 8-10 minutes). Let rest for 5-10 minutes out of the oven. Serve.

Harissa Pasta

Ingredients

- Pasta (2 cups)
- Red bell pepper (1)
- Red onion (1)
- Pine nuts (2 Tbsp.)
- Harissa paste (2 Tbsp.)

Instructions

1. Roast onions and peppers with olive oil at 400F for 20 minutes. Remove from oven and dice.
2. Prepare pasta to instructions on package. While pasta cooks, toast your pine nuts until browned in frying pan.
3. Drain pasta, leaving a touch of the water. Then, add in diced roasted veggies and harissa. Serve topped with pine nuts.

Chapter 6: 1-Hour-or-Less Meals

1 Hour Baked Cod

Ingredients

- Basil (0.5 tsp., dried)
- Bay leaf (1)
- Capers (1 small jar)
- Cod fillets (2 pounds)
- Fennel seeds (1 tsp., crushed)
- Garlic (1 clove, minced)
- Lemon juice (0.25 c., fresh)
- Olive oil (2 tsp)
- Onion (1, sliced)
- Orange juice (o.25 c., fresh)
- Orange peel (1 Tbsp.)
- Oregano (0.5 tsp., dried)
- Salt and pepper to personal preference
- White wine (1 c., dry)
- Whole tomatoes (16-oz. can, chopped and reserving juice)

Instructions

1. Warm oven to 375F.
2. In cast iron skillet, warm oil. Then, sauté your onion for 5 minutes. At this point, mix in all other ingredients but fish. Allow to simmer for 30 minutes.
3. Place fillets into skillet and top with most of the sauce. Allow to bake for 15 minutes until fish flakes.

Grilled Chicken Mediterranean Salad

Ingredients

- Artichoke hearts (0.33 c., chopped)
- Balsamic vinegar (2 Tbsp.)
- Basil (1 tsp, dried)
- Chicken breasts (3, cut into bite-sized chunks)
- Cucumber (0.75 c., diced)
- Feta cheese (0.25 c.)
- Garlic (1 clove, minced)
- Greek yogurt (2 Tbsp.)
- Green onions (0.25 c., chopped)

- Kalamata olives (3 Tbsp., sliced)
- Kosher salt (0.5 tsp)
- Lemon juice (3 Tbsp + 1 tsp.)
- Olive oil (3 Tbsp. + 2 Tbsp.)
- Onion powder (0.5 tsp)
- Parsley (0.5 tsp)
- Pesto (4 tsp)
- Pinch of red pepper
- Roasted red pepper (6 Tbsp., sliced)
- Romaine (4 c., chopped)
- Shiitake mushrooms
- Spinach (4 c., chopped)
- Tomato (0.75 c., diced)
- White wine vinegar (4 tsp)

Instructions

1. Create your salad. Each plate should have a bed of romaine and spinach, topped with cucumber, tomato, artichoke, peppers, olives, and cheese.
2. Combine your tsp of lemon juice, wine vinegar, and pesto in a jar and shake to combine. Then, add in yogurt and 2 Tbsp. oil, mixing well until well-incorporated.
3. Prepare your chicken. Let it marinade in a mixture of 3 Tbsp. lemon juice, balsamic vinegar, remaining oil, and all seasonings for at least 30 minutes. Soak some wooden skewers in water during this time.
4. Make kebabs out of chicken and mushroom, alternating bite of chicken and bite of mushroom until chicken is gone. Grill for 10 to 15 minutes until done.
5. Drizzle salad with the vinaigrette, then place a kebab atop each. Serve.

Lemon Herb Chicken and Potatoes One Pot Meal

Ingredients

- Baby potatoes (8, halved)
- Basil (3 tsp, dried)
- Bell pepper (1, seeds removed and wedged)
- Chicken thighs (4, skin and bone on)
- Garlic (4 large cloves, crushed)
- Kalamata olives (4 Tbsp., pitted)
- Lemon juice (1 lemon's worth)
- Olive oil (3 Tbsp.)
- Oregano (2 tsp, dried)

- Parsley (2 tsp, dried)
- Red onion (wedged)
- Red wine vinegar (1 Tbsp.)
- Salt (2 tsp)
- Zucchini (1 large, sliced)
- Lemons for garnish

Instructions

1. Combine juice from lemon, 2 Tbsp. olive oil, vinegar, seasonings, and garlic into dish. Pour half to reserve for later, then place chicken in half. Let sit for 15 minutes (or overnight if you would like to prep the day before)

2. Warm oven to 430F. Sear chicken in cast iron skillet in remaining olive oil, about 4 minutes per side. Drain all but 1 Tbsp. of fat.

3. Place all veggies around the thighs. Top with remaining marinade and combine well to cover everything.

4. Cover pan and bake for 35 minutes until soft and chicken is to temperature. Then, broil for 5 minutes or until golden brown. Top with olives and lemon to serve.

Vegetarian Mediterranean Quiche

Ingredients

- Butter (2 Tbsp.)
- Cheddar cheese (1 c., shredded)
- Eggs (4 large)
- Feta (0.33 c.)
- Garlic (2 cloves, minced)
- Kalamata olives (0.25 c., sliced)
- Milk (1.25 c.)
- Onion (1, diced)
- Oregano (1 tsp, dried)
- Parsley (1 tsp, dried)
- Pie crust (1, prepared)
- Red pepper (1, diced)
- Salt and pepper to personal preference
- Spinach (2 c., fresh)
- Sun dried tomatoes (0.5 c.)

Instructions

1. Soak sun-dried tomatoes in boiling water for 5 minutes before draining and chopping.
2. Prepare a pie dish with a crust, fluting the edges.
3. In a skillet, melt your butter, then cook your garlic and onions in it until they become fragrant. Combine in the red peppers for another 3 minutes until softened. Then, toss in your spinach, olives, and seasoning. Cook until the spinach wilts, about 5 minutes. Take it off of the heat and toss

in your feta and tomatoes. Then, carefully place mixture into the crust, spreading it into a nice, even layer.

4. Mix milk, eggs, and half of cheddar cheese together. Pour it into the crust. Then, top with cheddar.

5. Bake for 50 minutes at 375 f. until crust is browned and egg is done.

Herbed Lamb and Veggies

Ingredients

- Bell pepper (2, any color, seeds removed and cut into bite-sized chunks)
- Lamb cutlets (8 lean)
- Mint (2 Tbsp., fresh, chopped)
- Olive oil (1 Tbsp.)
- Red onion (1, wedged)
- Sweet potato (1 large, peeled, and chunked)
- Thyme (1 Tbsp., fresh, chopped)
- Zucchini (2, chunked)

Instructions

1. Assemble your veggies onto a baking sheet and coat with oil and black pepper. Bake at 400F for 25 minutes.
2. As veggies bake, trim fat from the lamb. Then, combine the herbs with a bit of freshly ground pepper. Coat the lamb in the seasoning.
3. Remove veggies, flip, and push to one side of pan. Then, arrange your cutlets onto the baking pan as well. Bake for 10 minutes, flip, then cook an additional 10 minutes. Combine well, then serve.

Chicken and Couscous Mediterranean Wraps

Ingredients

- Parsley (1 c., fresh and chopped)
- Olive oil (3 Tbsp.)

- Garlic (2 tsp, minced)

- Salt (pinch)

- Pepper (pinch)

- Chicken tenders (1 pound)

- Tomato (1, chopped)

- Cucumber (1, chopped)

- Spinach wraps (4 1o-inch)

- Water (0.5 c)

- Mint (0.5 c., fresh chopped)

- Lemon juice (0.25 c.)

- Couscous (0.33 c.)

Instructions

1. Cook couscous in boiling water according to directions on package.
2. Mix together your lemon juice, oil, garlic, salt and pepper, mint, and parsley.
3. Coat chicken in 1 Tbsp. of your mixture from previous step and top with a pinch of salt. Cook in skillet until completely cooked, usually just a few minutes per side.
4. Wait for chicken to cool, then chop into bites.
5. Pour the remainder of your parsley mixture into the couscous with cucumbers and tomato bits.
6. Place 0.75 c. of couscous mixture into a tortilla, then spread chicken atop it, rolling them up and serving.

Sheet Pan Shrimp

Ingredients

For shrimp

- Feta cheese (0.5 c.)

- Fingerling potatoes (2 c., halved)

- Green beans (6 oz., trimmed)

- Olive oil (3 Tbsp.)

- Pepper (1 tsp)

- Red onion (1 medium, sliced)

- Red pepper (1 medium, sliced)

- Salt (1 tsp)

- Shrimp (1 lb., deveined and peeled)

For Marinade

- Garlic (1 Tbsp., minced) Oregano (0.5 tsp)

- Greek yogurt (1 c.)

- Lemon juice (2 Tbsp.)

- Paprika (0.5 tsp)

- Parsley (2 Tbsp., chopped)

Instructions

1. Combine all marinade ingredients and set aside.
2. Take shrimp in a bowl with 0.5 c. of the marinade. Let them sit for 30 minutes.
3. During rest time, set up your baking sheet with foil or parchment, and prepare your veggies. Chop them up and toss onto baking sheet, drizzling them with the olive oil and giving them a quick sprinkle of salt and pepper. Bake for roughly 20 minutes at 400F, then remove from oven. Take out all green beans and set to the side.
4. Place shrimp in one layer across the pan and bake for an additional 10 minutes until shrimp is done. Serve with veggies and shrimp in bowls, topped with 2 Tbsp. feta and a spoonful of yogurt marinade.

Mediterranean Mahi Mahi

Ingredients

- Basil (6 leaves, freshly chopped)
- Capers (4 Tbsp.)
- Garlic (2 cloves, chopped)

- Italian seasoning (pinch)
- Kalamata olives (25, chopped)
- Lemon juice (1 tsp)
- Mahi mahi (1 pound)
- Olive oil (2 Tbsp.)
- Onion (o.5, chopped)
- Parmesan cheese (3 Tbsp.)
- Diced tomatoes (15 oz. can)
- White wine (0.25 c.)

Instructions

1. Warm olive oil in a pan and then cook onions until translucent. Toss in garlic and seasoning and stir to mix well. Then, add in your can of tomatoes, wine, olives, lemon, and roughly half of the chopped basil. Drop heat down and toss in parmesan cheese. Cook until bubbling.
2. Put fish into a baking pan, then top with the sauce. Bake for 20 minutes at 425 F until fish is to temperature.

Chapter 7: Slow Cooker Meals

Slow Cooker Mediterranean Chicken

Ingredients

- Bay leaf (1)
- Capers (1 Tbsp.)
- Chicken broth (0.5 c.)

- Chicken thighs (2 pounds, bone and skin removed)
- Garlic (3 cloves, minced)
- Kalamata olives (1 c.)
- Olive oil (1 Tbsp.)
- Oregano (1 tsp)
- Roasted red pepper (1 c.)
- Rosemary (1 tsp, dried)
- Salt and pepper to taste
- Sweet onion (1, thinly sliced)
- Thyme (1 tsp, dried)
- Optional fresh lemon wedges to juice for serving

Instructions

1. Sauté the chicken in olive oil to brown on both sides, then remove it from the pan. Then, sauté the onions and garlic as well until beginning to soften, roughly 5 minutes.
2. Put chicken, onion, garlic, and all other ingredients into a slow cooker and leave it to cook for 4 hours on low. Season to taste.

Slow Cooker Vegetarian Mediterranean Stew

Ingredients

- Carrot (0.75 c., chopped)
- Chickpeas (15 oz. can)
- Crushed red pepper (0.5 tsp)
- Fire-roasted diced tomatoes (2 14-oz. cans)
- Garlic (4 cloves, minced)
- Ground pepper (0.25 tsp)
- Kale (8 c., chopped)

- Lemon juice (1 Tbsp.)
- Olive oil (3 Tbsp.)
- Onion (1, chopped)
- Oregano (1 tsp)
- Salt (0.75 tsp)
- Vegetable broth (3 c.)
- Basil leaves (garnish)
- Lemon wedges (garnish)

Instructions

1. Mix tomatoes, onion, carrot, broth, seasonings, and garlic into the slow cooker. Cook on low for 6 hours.

2. Take out 0.25 c. of the liquid in the slow cooker after 6 hours and transfer it to a bowl. Take out 2 Tbsp. of chickpeas and mash them with the liquid until nice and smooth.

3. Combine mash, kale, juice from lemon, and whole chickpeas. Cook for about 30 minutes, until kale is tender, then serve garnished with the basil leaves and lemon wedges.

Vegetarian Slow Cooker Quinoa

Ingredients

- Arugula (4 c.)
- Chickpeas (1 15.5 oz. can, rinsed and drained)
- Feta cheese (0.5 c)
- Garlic (2 cloves, minced)
- Kalamata olives (12, halved)
- Kosher salt (0.75 tsp)
- Lemon juice (2 tsp)
- Olive oil (2.25 Tbsp.)
- Oregano (2 Tbsp., fresh and coarsely chopped

- Quinoa (1.5 c., uncooked)
- Red onion (1 c., sliced)
- Roasted red pepper (0.5 c., drained and chopped)
- Vegetable stock (2.25 c.)

Instructions

1. Mix your broth with the onion, garlic, quinoa, chickpeas, and 1.5 tsp of olive oil. Sprinkle half of the salt atop it. Mix and cook on low until quinoa is done, roughly 3 or 4 hours.
2. Turn off the slow cooker and mix well. In a separate bowl, combine remaining olive oil, salt, and lemon juice together. Then, mix that into the slow cooker, along with the peppers.
3. Combine in the arugula and leave until the greens start to wilt. Serve, topping with feta, oregano, and olives.

Slow-Cooked Chicken and Chickpea Soup

Ingredients

- Artichoke hearts (14 oz. can, drained and chopped)
- Bay leaf (1)
- Cayenne (0.25 tsp)
- Chicken thighs (2 lbs., skins removed)
- Cumin (4 tsp)
- Diced tomatoes (1 15-ounce can)
- Dried chickpeas (1.5 c., allow to soak overnight)
- Garlic cloves (4, chopped)
- Olives (o.25 c., halved)
- Paprika (4 tsp)
- Pepper (0.25 tsp)
- Salt (0.5 tsp)

- Tomato paste (2 Tbsp.)
- Water (4 c.)
- Yellow onion (chopped)
- Parsley or cilantro (garnish)

Instructions

1. Drain your soaked chickpeas and place them into your slow cooker (large preferred). Mix in the water, onions and garlic, tomatoes (undrained), tomato paste, and all seasonings. Combine well, then add in the chicken.
2. Leave it to cook for 8 hours at low, or 4 at high.
3. Remove the chicken and allow it to cool on a cutting board. At the same time, remove the bay leaf, then add in the artichoke and olives. Season with additional salt if necessary to taste. Chop up chicken, removing the bones, and then mix it back into the soup. Serve the soup with the parsley or cilantro garnishing the top.

Slow Cooked Brisket

Ingredients

- Beef broth (0.5 c.)
- Brisket (3 lbs.)
- Cold water (0.25 c.)
- Fennel bulbs (2, cored, trimmed, and cut into wedges)
- Flour
- Italian seasoning (3 tsp)
- Italian seasoning diced tomatoes (14.5 oz. can)
- Lemon peel (1 tsp., fine shreds)
- Olives (0.5 c.)
- Parsley for garnish
- Pepper (pinch)
- Salt (pinch)

Instructions

1. Trim meat, then season with 1 tsp Italian seasoning. Put it in slow cooker with the cut-up fennel on top.
2. Mix together the tomatoes, broth, peel, olives, salt and pepper, and the last of the Italian seasoning.
3. Cook at low for 10 hours, or high for 5.
4. Take meat out of the cooker and reserve all juice. Arrange meat with veggies on a serving platter.
5. Remove fat from top of the juices.
6. Take 2 c. of juices in saucepan. Mix together water and flour, then combine it into the juice. Cook until gravy forms.
7. Serve meat topped with gravy and garnish with parsley.

Vegan Bean Soup with Spinach

Ingredients

- Vegetable broth (3 14-oz. cans)
- Tomato puree (15 oz. can)
- Great Northern or White beans (15 oz. can)
- White rice (0.5 c)
- Onion (0.5 c., chopped)
- Garlic (2 cloves, minced)
- Basil (1 tsp., dried)
- Pinch of salt
- Pinch of pepper
- Kale or spinach (8 c., chopped)

Instructions

1. Mix everything but leafy greens together in your slow cooker. Cook for 5 or 7 hours on low, or 2.5 hours on high.
2. Toss in leafy greens. Wait for them to wilt and serve.

Moroccan Lentil Soup

Ingredients

- Carrots (2 c., chopped)
- Cauliflower (3 c.)
- Cinnamon (0.25 tsp)
- Cumin (1 tsp)
- Diced tomato (28 oz.)
- Fresh cilantro (0.5 c.)
- Fresh spinach (4 c.)
- Garlic (4 cloves, minced)
- Ground coriander (1 tsp)
- Lemon juice (2 Tbsp.)
- Lentils (1.75 c.)
- Olive oil (2 tsp)

- Onion (2 c., chopped)
- Pepper (pinch)
- Tomato paste (2 Tbsp.)
- Turmeric (1 tsp)
- Vegetable broth (6 c.)
- Water (2 c.)

Instructions

1. Mix everything but spinach, cilantro, and lemon juice. Cook until lentils soften. This will be 4-5 hours if you use high heat, or 10 hours on low.
2. Mix spinach when just 30 minutes remains on cook time.
3. Just before serving, top with cilantro and lemon juice.

Chapter 8: Vegetarian and Vegan Meals

Vegetarian Greek Stuffed Mushrooms

Ingredients

- Cherry tomatoes (0.5 c., quartered)

- Feta cheese (0.33 c.)

- Garlic (1 clove, mixed)

- Ground pepper (0.5 tsp)

- Kalamata olives (2 Tbsp.)

- Olive oil (3 Tbsp.)

- Oregano (1 Tbsp., fresh and roughly chopped)

- Portobello mushrooms (4, cleaned with stems and gills taken out)

- Salt (0.25 tsp)

- Spinach (1 c., chopped)

Instructions

1. Begin by setting your oven. This recipe requires 400F for baking.

2. Mix together your salt and 0.25 tsp pepper, garlic, and 2 Tbsp. of oil, and use it to cover your mushrooms, inside and out.

3. Set the mushrooms onto your baking pan and allow it to cook for 10 minutes.

4. Mix together your remaining ingredients and combine well. Then, when the mushrooms are done, remove them from the oven and then fill them up with your filling.

5. Allow to cook for another 10 minutes.

Vegetarian Cheesy Artichoke and Spinach Stuffed Squash

Ingredients

- Artichoke Hearts (10 oz., frozen—thawed and chopped up)
- Baby spinach (5 oz.)
- Cream cheese (4 oz., softened)
- Parmesan cheese (0.5 c.)
- Pepper (pinch to taste)
- Red pepper and basil (for garnish)
- Salt (pinch to taste)

- Spaghetti squash (1, cut in half and cleaned out of seeds)
- Water (3 Tbsp.)

Instructions

1. Microwave your squash, flat side down, with 2 Tbsp. of your water uncovered for 10-15 minutes.
2. Mix together your spinach and water into a skillet until they begin to wilt. Then drain and reserve for later.
3. Preheat your oven set to broil with the rack at the upper 1/3 point.
4. Remove flesh from squash with a fork, then place the shells onto a sheet for the oven. Then stir in your artichoke, cheeses, and a pinch of salt and pepper to the squash flesh. Combine thoroughly, then split it between the two shells. Broil for 3 minutes and top with red pepper and basil to taste.

Vegan Mediterranean Buddha Bowl

Ingredients

For the chickpeas

- Chickpeas (1 can, rinsed, drained, and skinned)
- Olive oil (1 tsp)
- Pinch of salt and pepper
- Dried basil (0.25 tsp)
- Garlic powder (0.25 tsp)

For the quinoa

- Quinoa (0.5 c.)
- Water (1 c.)

For the salad

- Bell pepper (1, color of choice, seeded, stemmed, and chopped to bite-sized bits)
- Cucumbers (2, peeled and chopped)
- Grape tomatoes (1 c., halved)
- Hummus (0.5 c.)
- Kalamata olives (0.5 c.)
- Lettuce (2 c. – can sub in field greens, spinach, kale, or any other leafy greens)

Instructions

1. Set your oven up to prepare for baking. It should be at 0400F. Then, mix the ingredients for the chickpeas together, coating them evenly with the seasoning.
2. Put chickpeas in single layer and put them onto the baking sheet. Roast for 30 minutes with an occasional mixing and rotation of the pan to allow them all to cook evenly. Allow them to cool.
3. Start preparing the quinoa and water in a microwave-safe bowl. Combine the water and quinoa and microwave, covered, for 4 minutes. Then stir and microwave for 2 minutes longer. Give it one final stir and leave it to rest in the microwave for another minute or two.
4. Begin assembling your salad. Begin with the greens at the bottom, then top with tomatoes, cucumbers, bell pepper, olives, chickpeas, and then quinoa. Finally, top with a dollop of hummus to serve.

Vegan Mediterranean Pasta

Ingredients

- Artichokes (0.5 c.)

- Basil leaves (0.25 c., torn)

- Garlic cloves (2-3 to taste, minced)

- Grape tomatoes (2 c., halved)

- Kalamata olives (10, pitted)

- Olive oil (1 Tbsp.)

- Pasta (8 oz.)

- Red pepper (o.25 tsp.)

- Salt and pepper to taste
- Spinach (4 c.)
- Tomato paste (4 Tbsp.)
- Vegetable broth (1 c.)

Instructions

1. Prepare your pasta based on the instructions provided. Keep 1 c. of the water for later use and then set the pasta aside.
2. While preparing your pasta, take the time to warm a large skillet with oil. Then, sauté your garlic and red pepper for 30 seconds or so. Combine in the tomato paste and cook for another minute. At that point, mix in your tomatoes, your seasoning, your artichokes and olives, and your broth. Let it cook until tomatoes start to break down.
3. Mix in the pasta to the tomato mixture. Let it cook another 2 minutes and add reserved pasta water if too dry.
4. Add in spinach and basil and cook until wilted.
5. Remove from heat and serve.

Vegetarian Zucchini Lasagna Rolls

Ingredients

- Basil (2 Tbsp., fresh)
- Egg (1, lightly beaten)
- Frozen spinach (10-ounce package, thawed and dried)
- Garlic (1 clove)
- Marinara sauce (0.75 c.)
- Olive oil (2 tsp)
- Parmesan cheese (3 Tbsp.)
- Pinch each of salt and pepper
- Ricotta (1.33 c.)
- Shredded mozzarella cheese (8 Tbsp.)
- Zucchini (2, trimmed)

Instructions

1. Prepare two baking sheets with cooking spray. Then set the oven to 425F.
2. Cut up your zucchini into strips lengthwise into 1/8 inch thick pieces. A mandolin will make this easier.
3. Prepare zucchini coated in oil with salt and pepper, then set up a flat layer across the bottom of the prepared pan.
4. Bake zucchini for 10 minutes until it begins to soften.
5. Mix together 2 Tbsp. mozzarella and 1 Tbsp. of parmesan. Then, in another bowl, combine egg, ricotta, spinach, garlic, and the remainder of the cheese. Toss in a pinch of salt and pepper and mix well.
6. Set up an 8-inch square casserole dish with 0.25 c. marinara spread across the bottom.
7. Take your zucchini that has been softened and begin to roll it. To do this, you will need to put 1 Tbsp. of ricotta mix at the bottom of your strip, then roll. Put the seam down in the marinara-covered bottom. Do this for all pieces of zucchini.
8. Cover the rolls with the remainder of your marinara sauce and top with the cheese mix.
9. Bake until bubbling, roughly 20 minutes. Rest for 5 minutes and top with basil.

Vegetarian Breakfast Sandwich

Ingredients

- Sandwich thins (2)
- Olive oil (2 Tbsp. + 1 tsp)
- Rosemary (1 Tbsp. fresh, or 0.5 tsp dried)
- Eggs (2)
- Spinach leaves (1 c.)

- Tomato (0.5, sliced thinly)
- Feta (2 Tbsp.)
- Pinch of salt and pepper

Instructions

1. Warm oven to 375F. Separate your sandwich thins and coat with olive oil. Bake for 5 minutes until beginning to crisp up.
2. Warm skillet with last tsp of olive oil. Break eggs into pan and cook until whites are set. Then, break the yolks and flip to finish cooking.
3. Put bottoms of the bread onto serving plates. Then, top with spinach, the tomato, one egg each, followed by the feta. Sprinkle with salt and pepper, then top with remaining bread.

Vegan Breakfast Toast

Ingredients

- Bread of choice (verify that it is vegan—2 slices)
- Spice blend of choice
- Arugula (handful)
- Tomato (1, cut into rounds)
- Chopped olives (1 Tbsp.)
- Cucumber (0.5, cut into rounds)
- Hummus (0.25 c.)

Instructions

1. Toast up your bread. Then spread the hummus across, season it, and top with all toppings split between the pieces.

Vegetarian Shakshouka

Ingredients

- Chopped parsley (1 Tbsp.)
- Diced Tomatoes (15 oz. can)
- Eggs (4)
- Garlic (2 cloves)

- Olive oil (2 Tbsp.)
- Onion (1—sliced)
- Red bell peppers (2, sliced thinly)
- Salt and pepper to taste
- Spicy harissa (1 tsp)
- Sugar (1 tsp)

Instructions

1. Warm oil in a cast iron pan. Sauté your peppers and onions until they have begun to soften, giving them a stir every now and then to prevent sticking. Add in the garlic for another minute.
2. Put in tomatoes, sugar, and harissa, leaving it to simmer for the next 7 minutes.
3. Season it to taste. Then, add in small indentations into the mixture in the pan, cracking an egg in each indentation that you make. Cover up the pot and allow it to cook until egg whites are done.
4. Cover with parsley and serve with bread.

PART II

Chapter 1: The Power of the Crock Pot and Its Benefits

The Ways You Can Benefit

Think of how many times you have experienced 'spells' that you did not feel like spending hours over the stove preparing dinner. Can you relate? How about the times during the holidays when you are planning on a houseful of guests; yikes? By the way, "Don't sweat it because you have your fabulous cooker and all of these new recipes to try out."

These are a few ways to make the path a bit easier:

Get Ahead of the Meal: Preparing food with your Crock-Pot® can put you ahead of the game the night before you have a busy day planned. You can always make the meal for the next day in just a few minutes. Put all of the ingredients (if they can combine overnight) into the pot, so when you get up the next morning; all you need to do is take it out of the fridge, and let it get to room temperature. Turn it on as you head out of the door and dinner will be ready when you get home. YES!

Save a lot of Effort and Time: All it takes is a few good recipes and a little bit of your valuable time. In most of the cases, these recipes are geared towards a fast lifestyle and will be ready with just a few simple steps. After some time and practice, you will know exactly which ones will be your favorites; all of them!

Cut Back on Dining Out: Having an enjoyable meal at home is so much more personal for your family because you (and your pot) prepared it! Not only that, You will eliminate the temptation to order foods that might not be so healthy and in turn—will be more expensive.

Watching the Extra Liquids: There is no need to use additional ingredients, other than what is described within each of the recipes. Ideally, you should not fill the more than half to two-thirds full of ingredients. Too much liquid will cause a leakage from the top and may result in improperly cooked food.

Cook it Slow & Leave it Alone: A slow cooker is known for creating delicious dishes while bringing out all of the natural flavors. So, go ahead and go to work or have some fun—or—better yet go to bed early! There is no need to worry about checking on it (unless the recipe calls for it). Each time the lid is removed—valuable heat is escaping—resulting in a breakdown of the advised times. Just keep that element it in mind, even though it smells so good!

Trimming the Fat: One huge advantage to the use of this type of cooking is you can save quite a chunk of money purchasing cheaper cuts of meat. Also, capitalize on the flavorful meat in small quantities and by bulking up on veggies with smaller meat portions.

Hot Antioxidants

Many recent studies have discovered cooking some food items such as tomatoes will increase the bioavailability of many of the nutrients. For example, lycopene which is linked to cancer and heart prevention becomes move available to the body because the heat releases the lycopene.

A study from 2003 compared the content of fresh, frozen, and canned corn which was processed with heat; specifically lutein and xeaxanthin, and found less lutein in the fresh version. This lutein is mostly well-known to protect you from some eye diseases.

Score 'ONE' for the Crock-Pot®.

Who Knew?

Basic Times & Settings

The question always arises of how long you should cook your items if you don't have a recipe for a Crock-Pot®. These are only general guidelines because the size of a pot will make a difference in the cooking times.

Regular Cooking Times	Crock Pot® High Temperatures	Crock Pot® Low Pot Temperatures
Hours		
1/4 to 1/2	1 to 2	4 to 6
1/2 to 1	2 to 3	5 to 7
1 to 2	3 to 4	6 to 8
2 to 4	4 to 6	8 to 12

Note: You must consider that root veggies take longer than other vegetables and meats which mean they should be placed in the lower part of the pot.

Are You Ready? Of course, you are!

Chapter 2: Healthy Breakfast Recipes

Boiled Eggs

Did you ever wake up in the middle of the night for a 'potty' break, and decided you want some boiled eggs or egg salad for breakfast or work tomorrow, but do not have the time to sit around and wait for the eggs to cook? You have a cure for that!

Ingredients and Instructions

The simplicity is amazing!

1) Pour some water into the Crock-Pot®, add as many eggs as you want, and set the pot for 3 ½ hours on the low setting. Go back to bed and enjoy tomorrow!

One-Hour Bread

Crave that fresh bread—no longer! You can have some delicious comfort food shortly!

Ingredients

1 ½ C. Baking Mix

3 Tbsp. Italian Seasoning

½ cup milk (skim is okay)

Optional: ½ C. shredded cheese or 3 Tbsp. Grated Parmesan cheese

Directions

1) Prepare the cooker with some non-stick cooking spray.

2) Combine all of the ingredients until the lumps are gone and empty into the cooker.

3) *Notes:* Bisquick® is a good choice.

Breakfast Fiesta Delight

Directions

1 Pound Country-Style Sausage

1 Package (28-ounces) frozen hash brown potatoes (thawed)

½ Cup whole milk

12 large eggs

1 ½ Cups shredded Mexican blend cheese

Directions

1) Prepare the Crock-Pot® by spraying it with some cooking spray to help with the cleanup.

2) Brown and crumble the sausage in a frying pan; remove and pat the grease away using a paper towel.

3) Whip the eggs together in a mixing container.

4) Layer the ingredients with a layer of potatoes, cheese, sausage, and eggs.

5) *Serving Time:* Have some salsa, sour cream, pepper, and salt for a tasty topping.

Servings: Six to Eight

Prep Time is fifteen minutes

Cooking Time is six to eight hours.

Italian Sausage Scramble

Ingredients

1 ½ Lbs. Italian sausage

1 medium yellow onion

6 medium red potatoes

¼ Cup fresh Italian minced parsley

One medium diced tomato

1 Cup frozen/fresh kernel corn

2 cups grated Cheddar cheese

Directions

1) Discard the outer casing from the sausage. Peel and dice the onions and potatoes.

2) Sauté the onion and crumbled sausage until browned. Place them on a few paper towels to absorb the grease/fat and add the items to the slow cooker.

3) Combine the rest of the ingredients—blending well. Cover and cook.

Servings: Six

Prep Time is 15 Minutes.

Cook Time: The high setting is for four hours, and the lower setting is for six to eight hours.

The Sweeter Side of Breakfast

Blueberry Steel Cut Oats

Ingredients

1 ½ C. of water

2 C. frozen blueberries

1 banana

1 C. Steel cut oats

1- ½ C. Vanilla almond milk

1 Tbsp. butter

1 ½ tsp. cinnamon

Directions

1) Prepare a six-quart cooker with the butter, making sure to cover the sides also.

2) Mash the banana slightly and add all of the ingredients into the Pot—stirring gently.

3) Place the top on the crock pot and cook for *one hour* on the HIGH setting; switch to the WARM setting overnight, and sleep tight!

Wake up ready for a busy day by adding a drizzle of honey and get moving!

Servings: Four to Six

Preparation Time: Fifteen Minutes

Cooking Time: Eight hours

Pumpkin Pie Oatmeal

Ingredients

1 C. oats (steel cut)

3 ½ C. water

1 C. pumpkin puree

¼ tsp. each:

- salt
- vanilla extract
- pumpkin pie spices

Optional: 2 Tbsp. maple syrup

Directions

1) Use some non-stick cooking spray to coat the Crock-Pot®.
2) Empty the oats into the Pot.
3) Mix the remainder of the ingredients in a large mixing container, and pour over the oats.
4) *Note:* If you like sweeter oatmeal just adjust the flavor after it is cooked.

Cooking Time: Eight hours on low

Pumpkin Butter

Ingredients

4 Cups pumpkin

1 tsp. ground ginger

2 tsp. cinnamon

1-¼ Cups honey/maple syrup

½ tsp. nutmeg

1 tsp. vanilla extract (*optional*)

Instructions

1) Blend the vanilla, syrup/honey, and pumpkin puree in the Crock-Pot®.

2) Cover and cook. During the last hour—add the ginger, cinnamon, and nutmeg.

3) If you want it a little thicker, you can crack the lid. After all, the aroma is tantalizing—especially first thing in the morning!

You can store in jars in the bottom of the fridge for a healthy addition—anytime.

Yields: About 10 ounces

Preparation Time: Five Minutes

Cooking Time: Five hours

Chapter 3: Time-Saving Lunch Specialties

Beef Tacos
Ingredients
1 Package taco seasoning
1 (ten-ounce) Can tomatoes and green chilies (Rotel)
1 Pound lean ground beef
Directions
1) Add everything listed into your Crock-Pot®.

2) If you are available; stir every couple of hours to break up the

    beef or break it up before serving.

3) Serve on a floured tortilla or taco shell with your choice of

    toppings.

Servings: 12 tacos
Preparation Time: Two Minutes
Cooking Time: Five to Six Hours

Root Beer & BBQ Chicken
Ingredients
1 (18-ounce) bottle barbecue sauce
4 chicken breasts
¼ teaspoon each pepper and salt
½ can or bottle root beer (full-sugar)
Note: You can use Dr. Pepper or Coke instead of root beer.
Directions
1) Pour the drink of choice, and place the chicken in the cooker.

2) Drain once the chicken has finished cooking, and discard most of

    the liquid—but leaving enough to prevent dryness.

3) Flavor with some pepper and salt if desired and empty the contents of the sauce into the Crock-Pot®, cooking for about 15 to 20 minutes.

4) Enjoy on some burger buns or rolls.

Cooking Time: The high temperature will have it ready in 3 hours.

Stuffed Banana Peppers

Ingredients
1 Package Italian Sausage
Banana Peppers
2 Jars of Marinara Sauce (approximately)
Directions

1) Adapt this for your crowd on the amounts used.

2) Remove both ends of the peppers and scoop out the seeds and discard them.

3) Pour ½ of the jar of sauce in the Crock-Pot®.

4) Dice the sausage, in case it is not already prepared.

5) Stuff the pepper with the sausage and put them into the Pot.

6) Pour the sauce over the banana peppers.

Cooking Time: Low for eight to nine hours

Crock-Pot® Taco Soup

Ingredients

1 (14.5-ounces) Can Each:

- Beef broth

- Petite diced tomatoes

1 (15-ounces) Can Each:

- Black beans

- Corn

1 (10-ounces) Can Rotel Original

1 Can kidney beans (16-ounces)

1 (1-oz.) pouch each:

- Taco seasoning mix

- Ranch seasoning mix (Hidden Valley)

½ teaspoon salt

1 ½ teaspoons onion powder

1 Lb. ground beef

Garnish: Sour Cream, Fritos, chopped green onions, or some shredded cheddar cheese

Notes: The recipe is excellent if you choose the 'Diced Tomatoes with Green Chilies.'

Directions

1) Cook the beef and drain. Rinse and drain all of the cans of veggies except for the chilies; reserve the liquid from the corn and tomatoes.

2) Toss everything into the Crock-Pot® (except for the garnishes).

3) Cook for the necessary time.

4) When the process is completed, add the garnishes of your choice with some Fritos on the side to complement the flavors

Servings: 8 to 10

Prep Time: Ten minutes

Cook Time: Low for 4 hrs. or High for 2 hrs.

Chapter 4: Dinner in a Hurry
Beef

Meat for the Tacos

Ingredients

2 Lbs. Ground beef (lean)

1 cup diced onions/Birds Eye Chopped Onions and Garlic

1 Package low-sodium taco seasoning mix

Directions

1) Put the burger into the Crock-Pot® and cook it for four to six hours. If you are in the area of the kitchen—stir the meat every couple of hours to ensure it is cooking evenly (if not—no worries).

2) When the cooking cycle is complete; drain the beef on some paper towels.

3) Combine the onions and ½ to one package of the taco seasoning.

4) Blend well and continue cooking for about one more hour

Servings: Six

Preparation Time: Five Minutes

Cooking Time: Low setting: Four to Six hours

Steak Pizzaiola

Ingredients

1 (one to two pounds) London Broil

1 Yellow, orange, or red sliced bell pepper

1 Large sliced onion

¼ Cup water

½ to ¾ of a jar (your choice) tomato pasta sauce

Directions

1) Flavor the meat with the pepper and salt and place it into the Crock-Pot®.

2) Add the peppers and onions, followed by your favorite sauce,

3) Cook for six to eight hours. (Flip a time or two if you are home.)

4) Serve over some pasta, potatoes, or veggies.

Cooking Time: Low heat for six to eight hours

Steaks in the Pot

Ingredients

4 to 6 steaks

¼ C. White Wine

2 T. A-1 Sauce

2 T. Dijon mustard

Directions

1) Blend the mustard and steak sauce; add it to each of the pieces of steak.

2) Add the meat into the Crock-Pot®, add the wine, and cook for six to eight hours.

Servings: Four or More

Cooking Time: 6 to 8 Hours on the low setting

Chicken and Turkey

Buffalo Chicken
Ingredients
3 to 5 Pounds (no skin or bones) chicken breasts
1 (12-ounce) Bottle Red Hot Wings Buffalo Sauce
1 Pouch ranch dressing mix
Directions

1) Put the chicken into the Crock-Pot®. Empty the sauce over the breasts and sprinkle the ranch mix over the top. Cover and Cook.

2) Take the chicken out of the Pot and throw away the sauce.

3) Shred the chicken with a couple of forks. It should be tender.

4) Put it back into the cooker and stir to coat the chicken thoroughly.

5) Leave it in the pot on low about one more hour. Most of the sauce will be absorbed.

Cooking Time: Low for five hours

Caesar Chicken

Ingredients
1 bottle (12-ounces) Caesar dressing
4 skinless & boneless chicken breasts
½ Cup shredded Parmesan cheese
Directions

1) Add the breasts of chicken to the Crock-Pot®.

2) Cook the chicken for the specified time and drain the juices.

3) Empty the dressing over the breasts.

4) Sprinkle the cheese on top of that and cook for thirty more minutes covered until done.

Have a side of Caesar salad to complement the meal.

Servings: Four

Prep Time: 5 minutes

Cooking Time: Use the low setting for 6 hrs. ; the high setting High for 3 hrs.

Cranberry Chicken

Ingredients

4 (no skin or bones) Chicken Breasts

1 (8-ounces) bottle Kraft Catalina dressing

1 Pouch dry onion soup
1 (14-ounces) Can Ocean Spray Whole Cranberry Sauce
Directions

1) Cook the chicken in the Crock-Pot® according to your specified

   times. Drain the juices.

2) Combine the cranberry sauce, onion soup mix, and dressing.

   Empty it over the chicken.

3) Cook—covered—about 30 minutes.

Servings: Four

Preparation Time: Five minutes

Cooking Time: High for three hours or low for six hours

French Onion Chicken

Ingredients

4 Chicken breasts (no bones or skin)

1 Can French Onion soup (10.5-ounces)
½ cup sour cream

Directions

1) Put the breasts in the Pot and cook for the stated time. Empty

   the liquids.

2) Combine the soup and sour cream and add into the pot on top of

   the chicken

breasts.

3) Cook covered for about 30 minutes.

Servings: Four
Preparation Time: Five Minutes
Cooking Time: The high setting will take approximately three hours, whereas the low setting takes six hours.

Hawaiian Chicken
Ingredients

4 to 5 skinless and boneless breasts of chicken (thawed)

1 (20-oz.) Can Dole Pineapple Chunks

1 Bottle (12-oz.) Heinz Chili Sauce

1/3 C. brown sugar

Directions

1) Cook the chicken until its predetermined time limit is completed.

   Empty the liquid.

2) Combine the brown sugar, ½ of the juices of the can of

pineapples, the chili sauce, and the chunks of pineapple.

3) Empty the mixture over the drained breasts and heat on the high

   setting for approximately 30 minutes or so.

4) Have a bit of pineapple in every bite. Yummy!

Servings: 4 to 5

Preparation Time: 5 min.

Cooking Time: High = 6 hrs. / Low = 3 hrs.

Honey Mustard Chicken

Ingredients
1 (12-ounces) Bottle Dijon mustard
1/3 C. honey
4 skinless & boneless chicken breasts (thawed)
Directions
1) Cook the chicken for its predetermined time and dispose of the

   juices.

2) Combine the mustard and honey in a small dish.

3) Empty the sauce over the chicken and cook for about ½ hour

   (covered) until done,

Servings: Four
Preparation Time: Five Minutes
Cooking Time: Use the low setting for six hrs. Or on high for three hrs.

Chicken Italian Style

Ingredients

4 chicken breasts (thawed – no bones- no skin)

1 (16-ounce) Bottle Italian Dressing

Directions

1) Place the breasts of chicken into your Crock-Pot® and pour the

   dressing on them.

2) Put the lid on and let it do your work!

Servings: Four

Preparation Time: 5 minutes

Cooking Time: Use the high setting to prepare the chicken for 3.5 hrs. Or use the low setting for 7 hours.

Swedish Meatballs

Ingredients

1 (12-ounce) jar Heinz HomeStyle Gravy (Savory Beef)

1 (eight-ounce) container of sour cream

1 Bag Frozen Meatballs

Instructions

1) Empty the gravy into the Crock-Pot®, followed by the sour

   cream.

2) Combine these until they are completely blended.

3) Toss the package of frozen meatballs into the Pot filling to

   approximately 2/3 to ¾ of the space.

4) Place the lid on the pot and cook—occasionally stirring if you

   happen to be close to the kitchen.

5) You can always make more or less of the recipe depending on how many people you will serve.

Cooking Time: Low for a minimum of 5 hours

Sweet and Sour Chicken

Ingredients
1 (22-ounces) Bag frozen Tyson Chicken Breast
2 Cups cooked rice/steamed vegetables (or both)
1 bottle (18-ounces) Apricot Preserves
1 jar (12-ounces) chili sauce
Directions
1) Layer the frozen chicken pieces into the Crock-Pot®.

2) Combine the preserves and chili sauce in a small container (a mixing cup is ideal). Empty it over the chicken. *Note:* You can also use pineapple or a combination.

3) Toss to mix and let the Pot do the work.

4) Enjoy with some veggies and rice.

Servings: Six (one cup per serving)
Cooking Time on the high setting is 2 to 3 hours.

Creamy Taco Chicken

Ingredients
1 Can Rotel Original Tomatoes with Green Chilies
3 chicken breasts (no bone or skin)
4-ounces cream cheese (regular or light)
Directions

97

1) Pour the tomatoes, and place the chicken into the slow cooker.

2) A few minutes before the end of the cooking cycle, use a fork or tongs to shred the chicken.

3) Put the cream cheese on top of the mixture, but don't stir.

4) By the time the meal is ready, the cheese will be oozing into your chicken. Yummy!

Suggestions: You can use this in a casserole, over rice, as a salad, or any other creative plan you may have for your meal.
Cooking Time: Low temperature - Six to Eight hours

Stuffed – Roasted Turkey
Ingredients
2 C. Stuffing Mix
Black pepper and salt
6 Pounds Turkey
1 Tablespoon melted butter
Instructions
1) Use the package instructions to prepare the stuffing.

2) Flavor the turkey with some melted butter, pepper, and salt.

3) Prepare the bird by loosely placing the stuffing in the carcass.

4) Cover and let the Pot do the rest.

Servings: Four
Cooking Time: Low: 9 to 11 hours; High: 5 hours

Fish

Citrus Flavored Fish

Ingredients
Pepper and Salt
1 ½ pounds fish fillets
1 medium chopped onion
4 tsp. oil
5 Tbsp. Chopped parsley
2 tsp. Each grated: lemon and orange rind
Garnish: Lemon and orange slices
Directions
Use some butter to grease the Crock-Pot®.

1) Flavor the fish with some pepper and salt and put it into the pot.

2) Add the parsley, grated rinds, and onion as well as the oil over the fish.

3) Cover and cook.

4) When ready to eat; garnish with some lemon or orange slices.

Cooking Time: 1 ½ Hours on Low

Salmon Bake

Ingredients

3 (one-pound) Cans Salmon

1 (16-ounces) can tomato puree

4 cups bread crumbs (10 slices worth)

1 chopped green pepper

3 teaspoons lemon juice

2 crushed chicken bouillon cubes

1 Can each (condensed) cream of onion soup & cream of celery soup

6 (well-beaten) eggs

½ cup milk

Directions

1) Use some cooking spray or other oil to grease the Crock-Pot®
   lightly.

2) Blend all of the ingredients—except for the milk and celery soup
   into the Pot.

3) Cover and cook.

4) Combine and stir the milk and celery soup in a small pan to use
   as a sauce for the salmon.

5) When the salmon is done, garnish and enjoy with the special
   sauce!

Cooking Time: High for three hours or low for four to six hours

Pork

BBQ Style Pork Steaks
Ingredients

4 (½-inch cut) Pork shoulder steaks

2 large sliced tomatoes

1 large onion

1 large thinly sliced bell pepper

1 Tbsp. Each:

- Vegetable oil

- Tapioca (quick-cooking)

¼ C. red wine

½ tsp. cumin

½ C. barbecue sauce (your choice)

Directions

1) Slice and cut the onion as if you are preparing to make onion

   rings for dinner.

2) Trim away an excess fat and slice the steaks in half - lengthwise.

3) Brown the steaks in skillet using hot oil, and drain on paper

   towels.

4) Organize the peppers, tomatoes, and onions in the Crock-Pot®;

   sprinkling the tapioca over them. Place the pork in last.

5) Prepare the cumin, wine, and barbecue sauce in a small dish. Pour

   it over the ingredients in the Pot, and cover.

Servings: Four

Cooking Time: Low Heat – Six to Eight Hours (or until veggies and meat are tender)

Note: The recipe is based on a 3 ½- or a 4-quart Crock-Pot®. If you have a different size the cooking time may vary.

Pepsi® Roast

Ingredients

1 Can Cream of mushroom soup

5 Lb. Pork Roast/ Steak/Chops

½ package dry onion soup mix

1 can Regular Pepsi (Don't use Diet)

Directions

1) Put the meat in the Crock-Pot® first and sprinkle with the soup

   mix.

2) Empty the mushroom soup and Pepsi over the meat.

3) Close the lid and let the pot do the rest of the chore.

Suggestion: Use the sauce to pour over some rice or potatoes.

Servings: Eight

Cooking Time: Low setting for six to seven hours

Ranch Chops

Ingredients

Pouch – Ranch Dressing Mix

Pork Chops

1 Can Cream of Chicken Soup Plus (+) 1 Can Water OR 2 Cups Cream of Chicken

Directions

1) Pour the liquids into the Crock-Pot® along with the chops and

   dressing mix.

Cooking Time: Use the low-temperature setting for four to six hours.

Ham in Cider Gravy

This ham is so tasty it cannot remain in the 'breakfast only' slot. It is so tasty and can advance to lunch and dinner menus as well.

Ingredients

1 (one to four pound) Ham

¾ cup maple syrup

2 cups unsweetened apple cider

3 Tablespoons cornstarch

Directions

1) Arrange the ham in the Crock-Pot® and top it off with the syrup and cider.

2) Cook until the time indicated below is completed.

3) Move the ham to a serving platter. Pour the liquid into a large cup (a measuring cup is perfect).

4) Whisk ½ of the cider and the cornstarch on the stovetop using the low-temperature setting until it is smooth. Continue whisking and increase the burner to med-low—adding small amounts of cider at a time—until the gravy is bubbly and thickened to the desired consistency.

Servings: Four to Eight

Preparation Time: Four minutes

Cooking Time: Low - six to eight hours

Casseroles

Crock-Pot® Dinner: Beef or Chicken

Ingredients

1 Whole/cut up chicken –or- legs and thighs OR a Beef Roast

2 Carrots

4 Potatoes

5 Ounces water

1 Can celery or cream of mushroom soup (10 ¾ ounce)

Directions

1) Cut the carrots into four-inch chunks. Put all of the ingredients

   into the Crock-Pot®.

2) Set the Pot and let it 'go.'

Servings: Four

Cooking Time: The high setting will cook the meal in six hours, or you can cook it all day using the low-temperature setting.

Squash 'N Chops

Ingredients

5 Pork (boneless) Port cutlets or chops

2 medium oranges

1 ¼ Pounds delicate/butternut squash

1/8 tsp. Ground red pepper

½ tsp. Garlic salt

¼ tsp. Each: Ginger, cloves, and cinnamon

Directions

1) Peel and slice the oranges. Peel and slice the squash lengthwise

   and discard the seeds. Cut the 'half' into sections ½-inches thick.

2) Flavor the pork with some garlic salt and red peppers. Use a 4- to 5- quart Crock-Pot® and place the chops/cutlets in the bottom.

3) Combine the ginger, cinnamon, and cloves in a small dish.

4) Top off the pork with the oranges along with the toppings in step 3.

5) Cover and cook.

Servings: 5

Cooking Time: Low for 4 hours

Lasagna Enchantment

This one has a few more steps, but it is so worth it—and it's easy.

Ingredients

2 Cans diced tomatoes (28-ounces) drained

Four finely chopped clove of garlic

2 Tbsp. oregano

½ tsp. salt

15-ounces fresh ricotta

¼ tsp. pepper

½ tsp. salt

½ C. shredded Parmesan cheese

1 (12-ounce) Package uncooked lasagna noodles

½ tsp. fresh (finely chopped) parsley – more if desired

2 C. spinach leaves (bagged is okay)

2 C. shredded Mozzarella cheese

Directions

1) Mix the garlic, drained tomatoes, pepper, salt, and oregano in a mixing container.

2) In another bowl, blend the parsley, Parmesan, and ricotta cheese.

3) Dip anywhere from 1/3 to ½ cup of the tomato combination on the base of the Crock-Pot®.

4) Layer the noodles, spinach, several dollops of the ricotta combo, and 1/3 to about ½ of the tomato combination. Sprinkle the mozzarella on the top of that section. Continue the process with the mozzarella on the top.

5) Close the lid on the Pot and let it do the work.

Servings: Six to Eight
Prep Time: 20 Minutes
Cook Time: High is 2 Hrs. or Low is 3 to 4 Hrs.

Sweet Potato Casserole

Ingredients
1 ½ C. applesauce
1 tsp. ground cinnamon
3 Tbsp. Margarine/butter
½ C. Toasted chopped nuts
2/3 C. Brown sugar
6 medium sweet potatoes

Directions
1) Peel and slice the potatoes cutting them into ½-inch bits and drop them into a 3 ½-quart Crock-Pot®.

2) In a separate dish, mix the brown sugar, cinnamon, melted butter, and applesauce. *Note*: Be sure you pack the brown sugar tight when it is measured.

3) Empty the mixture over the potatoes in the Pot.

4) When the potatoes are tender; you can top with the chopped nuts. Yummy!

Cooking Time: Six to Eight hours

Sides/Veggies

Slow Cooked Baked Potatoes
Ingredients

6 Baking Potatoes

Kosher Salt

Oil

Garnishes: Your choice

Directions

1) Prepare the potatoes with a good scrub and rinsing, but do not dry them.

2) Put each one in some foil while poking holes in each one using a fork.

3) Use a small amount of oil to drizzle over each one adding a sprinkle of salt, and close the foil.

4) To keep them from getting soggy, ball up several wads of foil into the cooker.

5) Layer the potatoes on the balls and cover. Leave them on warm in the Crock-Pot® until ready to serve.

Cooking Time: Low – Six to Eight Hours

Corn on the Cob

Ingredients

3 ears or 5 to 6 halves – Corn on the cob

Salt as needed

1/2 stick or ¼ cup of softened butter

Directions

1) Shuck and remove the silks from the corn; break them into halves.

2) Cover each one with butter and wrap individually in foil.

3) Wad some foil balls up in the base of the unit and add about 1-inch of water.

4) Put the potatoes into the Crock-Pot®, and cook for the allotted time.

Servings: 4

Preparation Time: Five minutes

Cooking Time: Use the high setting for two hours. *Note:* The cooking time may vary if you prepare the corn with another unit besides a 5 to 6-quart pot.

Ranch Mushrooms

Ingredients

½ Cup Melted butter

1 Pound fresh mushrooms

1 Package - ranch salad dressing mix

Instructions

1) Leave the mushrooms whole and wash them well.

2) Put them into the Crock-Pot®, adding the oil and ranch mix by drizzling it over the mushrooms.

3) Cover the Pot. It is best to stir once after hour one to blend the butter.

Servings: Six

Cooking Time: Low will have your mushrooms ready in three to four hours.

Sweet Potatoes

Ingredients

4 medium sweet potatoes

Optional Garnishes:

Brown Sugar, Butter, Mini Marshmallows

Directions

1) Clean and prepare the potatoes—thoroughly dry.

2) Use a fork and poke holes in each one, and double wrap them in

aluminum foil.

3) Put them in the Crock-Pot®--cooking them the specified amount of time. If you are close to the kitchen; turn and flip the potatoes in the pot occasionally.

4) Once they are done, add the garnishes of your choice and serve.

Servings: Four

Preparation Time: Five Minutes

Cooking Time: The Low setting is used for 8 hrs. or the High setting for 4 hrs. (Times may vary depending on the size of the potatoes, but you will know when they are ready by how soft the potato is when you give it a squeeze.)

Chapter 5: Desserts – Snacks & Treats to Devour

Apple Dump Cake

Ingredients

Butter (1 Stick)

Yellow cake mix (1 box)

Apple pie filling (1 Can)

Directions

1) Empty the apple filling into the Crock-Pot®.

2) *Dump* in the mix and then the butter on top of the mix.

Cooking Time: Cook the cake in the Pot on the low setting for approximately four hours for best results.

Enjoy!

Applesauce

Ingredients

12 Apples

1 teaspoon juice (+) ¼ of the lemon peel

2 cinnamon sticks

Directions

1) Peel, core, and slice the apples. Put the apples, lemon peel, and sticks into the Crock-Pot®.

2) Provide a drizzle to the top with the juice and set the cooking timer.

3) When the treat is ready—throw the lemon peel and cinnamon sticks into the garbage.

4) Blend with a regular or immersion blender.

5) Chill for a few hours.

Cooking Time is five to seven hrs.

Peach Cobbler
Ingredients
1 White cake mix (not prepared)
6 Large peaches
1- Stick (½- Cup) softened butter
Directions

1) Peel and slice the peaches, and put them into the Crock-Pot®.

2) Blend the butter and cake mix using a pastry blender. You want a

   crumbly texture.

3) Sprinkle the mix over the peaches, and cook.

Enjoy with a bowl of ice cream.
Servings: Eight
Preparation Time: Fifteen minutes
Cooking Times on the high setting is two to three hours; whereas the Low cycle
will extend for about four hours.

Cocktail Franks – Sweet and Sour
Ingredients

40- Ounces Pineapple chunks

2 Pounds cocktail franks

1 Cup each:

- Grape jelly

- Chili sauce

3 Tablespoons each:

- Prepared mustard

- Lemon juice

Directions

1) Mix the jelly, chili sauce, mustard, and lemon juice in the Pot, mixing it well.

2) Cover and use the high setting for fifteen to twenty minutes to blend the ingredients

3) Slice the franks into bite-sized pieces and add to the Crock-Pot®.

4) Pour in the drained chunks of pineapple.

Servings: 10

Cooking Times: *High* setting for two hours; *Low* setting for four hours.

PART III

Chapter 1: Introduction to the Heart-Healthy Diet

A heart-healthy diet is incredibly important. The truth is, you must be able to manage your diet well if you want to be healthy. The average diet is actually incredibly unhealthy for the heart, and the sooner that you are able to change up how you treat yourself and your body, the better off you will be. The average person consumes far too much salt and not enough of the important fruits and veggies that they need. As a result, they wind up with problems with their blood sugars, their blood pressure, and cholesterol levels. It is important to understand that your heart is one of the most important parts of your body—you cannot live without it. You need to keep it healthy. If you want to ensure that you can keep yourself healthy, you need to make sure that you eat the foods that will help you to nourish it readily. The sooner that you can do so, the better off you will be. This book is here to provide you with plenty of heart-healthy meals that you can enjoy that will help you to stay as healthy as possible.

The Rules of the Heart-Healthy Diet

Before we begin, let's go over some of the most important rules that go into the heart-healthy diet. These are rules that will help you to ensure that your body is kept as healthy as possible with foods that will nourish you well. Now, on this diet, you can expect to follow these rules:

1. **Decrease saturated and trans fats:** These are fats that are no good for anyone. Instead, it is recommended that you focus entirely on monounsaturated and polyunsaturated fats. These come from primarily

vegetarian options—common sources include olive and canola oils, avocado, nuts, and fatty fish.

2. **Increase fruits and veggies:** Your body needs the vitamins and minerals in fruits and veggies to stay as healthy as possible. You should be consuming at least seven to nine servings per day to keep your body healthy and on track.

3. **Consume more fiber:** Typically, on this diet, you want to up your fiber intake. Fiber is necessary to keep your body regular. It also helps with the way that you will naturally digest and absorb nutrients. You need both soluble and insoluble sources to stay as healthy as possible. Soluble fiber will aid in regulating your body and is fantastic for the heart. Insoluble fiber is there to help you regulate your weight and pass waste.

4. **Make the switch to plant proteins whenever possible:** You will also see that this diet advocates for more vegetarian options and less meat. While you can still eat meat, it is highly recommended that you choose to put in at least three servings of vegetable proteins, and you limit red meats down to just once a week. Twice a week, you should eat skinless poultry, and twice a week, you should enjoy fish.

5. **Up your whole grain intake:** This is essential to ensuring that you are not just consuming a bunch of empty carbs that aren't doing anything for you. By shifting to whole grains, you get more of the fiber that you need, and they are also usually full of better nutritional content as well.

6. **Limiting sweets:** If you are going to enjoy sweets, it is usually recommended that you cut out sugar or sugar-sweetened dishes. While

you do not have to completely eliminate them, you should, at the very least, monitor and regulate intake.

7. **Low-fat dairy products:** You should have between two and three servings of dairy per day, but they ought to be reduced fat.

8. **Drink in moderation:** Alcohol is okay—but is not really encouraged either. If you must drink alcohol, make sure that you do so in moderation, which is typically defined as no more than one per day for women and no more than two per day for men.

The Benefits of the Heart-Healthy Diet

The heart-healthy diet has all sorts of benefits that are worth enjoying, and you should be able to treat these as motivation. If you find that you are struggling to enjoy this diet, consider these benefits to give you that added boost. Ultimately, the heart is the key to the body, and if you can keep it healthier, you will enjoy a better life for reasons such as:

- **Preventing heart disease:** When you limit salts, sweets, red meats, and everything else, you will help your heart remain healthier, and in doing so, you will reduce your risk of both stroke and heart disease.

- **Keeping your body healthier:** This diet is often recommended to older people, and this is for good reason—it keeps the body more agile by reducing the risk of frailty and muscle weakness.

- **Cutting the risk of Alzheimer's disease:** This diet helps your cholesterol, blood sugar, and blood vessel health, all of which are believed to aid in reducing the risk of both dementia and Alzheimer's disease.

- **Cutting the risk of Parkinson's disease:** Similarly, because this diet will be high in antioxidants, it has been found to cut the risk of Parkinson's disease significantly.

- **Longer lifespan:** This diet, because it lowers your risk of heart disease and cancer, is actually able to reduce your risk of death by around 20%.

- **Healthier mind:** If you suffer from anxiety or depression, this diet can actually help to alleviate some of the symptoms, or keep them at bay in the future. Between the healthy fats, rich vegetable content, and the boost to your gut bacteria, you will find that your body and mind both are healthier than ever.

- **It helps manage weight:** If you have struggled with your weight for some time, you may find that using this diet will actually help you to manage it, thanks to the fact that you'll be cutting out much of the foods that tend to lead to weight gain in the first place. You'll be able to enjoy a healthier body as the weight fades away through enjoying this diet.

Chapter 2: Heart-Healthy Savory Meals

Shrimp Scampi and Zoodles

Ingredients

- Butter (1 Tbsp., unsalted)
- Dry white wine (0.5 c.)
- Garlic (4 cloves, grated)
- Lemon juice (2 Tbsp.)
- Lemon zest (1 Tbsp.)
- Linguini (6 oz.)
- Olive oil (2 Tbsp.)
- Parsley (0.25 c., chopped)
- Red pepper flakes (0.25 tsp.)
- Shrimp (1.5 lbs., peeled and deveined—preferably large)
- Zucchini (3, spiralized)

Instructions

1. Start by preparing the pasta based on the instructions on the package. Keep 0.25 c. of the water to the side and drain the rest. Put pasta back in the pot.
2. Combine the shrimp, garlic, oil, salt, and pepper to taste and allow it to sit for five minutes.
3. Prepare a skillet and cook your shrimp in the garlicky oil over medium and garlic until done, roughly 3-4 minutes per side with a large count. Move shrimp to plate without the oil.
4. Add zest and pepper to the oil, along with the wine. Scrape the brown bits and reduce to 50%. Mix in lemon juice and butter, then toss the zoodles in.
5. After 2 minutes, add in shrimp, pasta, and combine well. Mix in water if necessary and toss with parsley.

Citrus Chicken Salad

Ingredients

- Baby kale (5 oz.)

- Chicken thighs (2 lbs.)

- Dijon mustard (1 tsp)

- Lemon juice (2 Tbsp.)

- Olive oil (2 Tbsp.)

- Orange (1, cut into 6 pieces)

- Salt and pepper

- Stale bread (8 oz., torn up into bite-sized bits)

Instructions

1. Warm oven to 425F. As it preheats, warm up half of your oil into a skillet. Then, salt and pepper the chicken, cooking it skin-side down in the oil. After 6 or 7 minutes, when the skin is golden, remove it to a baking sheet. Then, toss in the orange wedges and roast another 10 minutes until the chicken is completely cooked.

2. Reserve 2 Tbsp. of the chicken fat in the pot and then return it to low heat. Toss in the bread chunks, coating them in the fat. Add a quick sprinkle of salt and pepper, then cook until toasted, usually about 8 minutes or so. Set aside.

3. Warm pan on medium-low, then toss in lemon juice. Deglaze the pan for a minute, then remove from heat. Combine with Dijon mustard and juice from roasted oranges. Mix in remaining oil.

4. Add kale and croutons to skillet to mix well, coating it in the mixture. Serve immediately with chicken.

Shrimp Taco Salad

Ingredients

- 3 Fresh lime juice (3 tbsp.)
- Avocado (1)
- Cayenne pepper sauce (1 tsp.)
- Cilantro leaves (1 c.)
- Corn chips (such as Fritos-- 2 c.)
- Extra-virgin olive oil (0.25 c.)
- Fresh corn (3 pieces)
- Ground coriander (0.25 tsp.)
- Ground cumin (0.25 tsp.)
- Salt
- Shrimp (1 lb.)
- Watermelon (2 c.)
- Zucchini (2 medium)

Instructions

1. Set up your grill to medium heat.
2. First grill the corn until it begins to char, usually about 10 minutes, with the occasional turn. At the same time, allow zucchini to grill for around 6 minutes until beginning to soften. Shrimp requires 2-4 minutes until cooked through, flipping once.
3. Combine your oil, juice, and seasonings, with just a pinch of salt.
4. Remove the kernels off of your corn and slice up your zucchini. Place zucchini and avocado onto a plate, topping it with the corn, then the watermelon, and finally the shrimp. You can leave it as is until you're ready to eat—it keeps for about a day in the fridge.
5. To serve, top with the chips (crumbled) and the dressing mix.

Chicken, Green Bean, Bacon Pasta

Ingredients

- Bacon (4 slices)
- Chicken breast (1 lb., cut into bite-sized bits)
- Egg yolk (1 large)
- Green beans (fresh—8 oz., trimmed and cut in half)
- Half-and-half (2 Tbsp.)
- Lemon juice (2 Tbsp.)
- Parmesan cheese (1 oz., grated—about 0.5 c.)
- Penne pasta (12 oz.)
- Scallions (2, sliced thinly)

- Spinach (5 oz.)

Instructions

1. Prepare pasta according to the package. Then, at the last minute of cooking, toss in the beans. Drain, reserving 0.5 c. of the cooking water. Leave pasta mix in the pot.
2. In a skillet, start preparing the bacon until crisp. Dry on a paper towel and then break into bits when cooled. Clean pan, reserving 1 Tbsp. of bacon fat.
3. On medium heat, cook the chicken until browning and cooked all the way. Then, off of the burner, toss in the lemon juice.
4. Mix together your egg and half-and-half in a separate container. Then, dump it to coat in the pasta and green beans, then toss in the chicken, spinach, and cheese. Mix well to coat. Add pasta water if needed, 0.25 c. at a time. Mix in the scallions, then top with bacon. Serve.

Ingredients

- Blackening seasoning (2 tsp.)
- Buttermilk (0.5 c.)
- Chicken drumsticks (2 lb., skinless)
- Cornflakes (4 c.)
- Olive oil (1 Tbsp.)
- Parsley (0.5 c., chopped)
- Salt (a pinch to taste)

Instructions

1. Get ready to bake the chicken at a temperature of 375F and make sure that you've got something to bake on that is currently protected.
2. Mix buttermilk, seasoning, and a touch of salt.
3. Crush cornflakes and put them in a second bowl. Combine with the oil and parsley.
4. Prep chicken by dipping first in buttermilk, letting it drip, then coating in cornflakes. Bake for 30-35 minutes.

Turkey Burgers and Slaw

Ingredients

Slaw

- Apple (1, matchstick-cut)
- Cabbage (8 oz., thinly sliced)
- Honey (1 Tbsp.)
- Jalapeno (1, thinly sliced and seeded)
- Lime juice (3 Tbsp.)
- Red wine vinegar (1 Tbsp.)
- Salt and pepper, to your preference

Burgers

- Buns (4, toasted lightly)

- Chili paste (1.5 Tbsp.)

- Ginger (1 Tbsp., grated)

- Olive oil (2 Tbsp.)

- Onion (0.5 chopped)

- Soy sauce (1 Tbsp.)

- Turkey (1 lb., ground up)

Instructions

1. Mix together the liquids for the slaw and the seasoning. Mix well, then toss in the slaw ingredients. Set aside.

2. Prepare your burger mixture, adding everything together, but the oil and the buns somewhere that you can mix them up. Combine well, then form four patties.

3. Prepare to your preference. Grills work well, or you choose to, you could use a cast iron pan with the oil. Cook until done.

4. Serve on buns with slaw and any other condiments you may want.

Slow Cooked Shrimp and Pasta

Ingredients

- Acini di pepe (4 oz., cooked to package specifications)
- Basil (0.25 c., chopped fresh)
- Diced tomatoes (14.5 oz. can)
- Feta (2 oz., crumbled)
- Garlic (2 cloves, minced)
- Kalamata olives (8, chopped)
- Olive oil (1 Tbsp.)
- Pinch of salt
- Rosemary (1.5 tsp fresh, chopped)
- Shrimp (8 oz., fresh or frozen)
- Sweet red bell pepper (1, chopped)
- White wine (0.5 c.) or chicken broth (o.5 c.)
- Zucchini (1 c., sliced)

Instructions

1. Thaw, peel, and devein shrimp. Set aside in fridge until ready to use them.
2. Coat your slow cooker insert with cooking spray, then add in tomato, zucchini tomatoes, bell pepper, and garlic.
3. Cook on low for 4 hours, or high for 2 hours. Mix in shrimp. Then, keep heat on high. Cook covered for 30 minutes.
4. Prepare pasta according to the instructions on the packaging.
5. Mix in the olives, rosemary, basil, oil, and salt.
6. Serve with pasta topped with shrimp, then topped with feta.

Chapter 3: Heart-Healthy Sweet Treats

Chocolate Mousse

Ingredients

- Avocado (1 large, pitted and skinned)
- Cocoa powder (2 Tbsp., unsweetened)
- Nondairy milk of choice (3 Tbsp., unsweetened)
- Nonfat vanilla Greek yogurt (0.25 c.)
- Semi-sweet baking chocolate (2 oz., melted and cooling)
- Sweetener packet if desired.
- Vanilla extract (1 tsp.)

Instructions

1. Prepare by putting all ingredients but sugar into a food processor. Combine well. Taste. If you want it sweeter, add in some sweetener as well.
2. Chill in your fridge until you are ready to serve.

Baked Pears

Ingredients

- Almonds (0.25 c., chopped)
- Brown sugar (0.33 c., can sub with honey)
- Butter (2 oz., melted, or coconut oil if you prefer vegan)
- Ground cinnamon (1 tsp)
- Ripe pears (3)
- Rolled oats (0.5 c.)
- Salt (a pinch)
- Sugar (pinch)

Instructions

1. Set oven to 400 F.
2. Incorporate all dry ingredients. Then, mix half of your melted butter.
3. Cut your pears in half and carve out the cores, making a nice scoop in the center. Brush with butter, then top with a sprinkle of sugar.
4. Put your cinnamon oat mixture into the centers of the pears.
5. Bake for 30-40 minutes, until soft.

Chocolate Peanut Butter Bites

Ingredients

- Chocolate chips of choice (2 c.)
- Coconut flour (1 c.)
- Honey (0.75 c.)
- Smooth peanut butter (2 c.)

Instructions

1. Prepare a tray with parchment paper to avoid sticking or messes
2. Melt together your peanut butter and honey, mixing well
3. Add coconut flour to peanut butter mixture and combine to incorporate. If it's still thin, add small amounts of flour. Let it thicken for 10 minutes.
4. Create 20 balls out of the dough.
5. Melt chocolate, then dip the dough balls into the chocolate and place them on the parchment. Refrigerate until firm.

Oatmeal Cookies

Ingredients

- Applesauce (2.5 Tbsp.)
- Baking soda (0.25 tsp)
- Coconut oil (2 Tbsp., melted)
- Dark chocolate chips (0.25 c.)
- Honey (0.25 c.)
- Salt (0.5 tsp)
- Vanilla extract (2 tsp.)
- Whole grain oats (0.5 c.)
- Whole wheat flour (0.5 c.)

Instructions

1. Set your oven to 350 F.
2. Mix syrup, oil (melted), applesauce, and vanilla.
3. Toss in salt, baking soda, oats, and flour. Combine well until it becomes a dough.
4. Mix the chocolate chips in.
5. Put in tablespoons onto cookie sheet.
6. Bake for 10 minutes. Let cool before transferring to a cooling rack.

Pina Colada Frozen Dessert

Ingredients

- Butter (0.25 c.)
- Crushed pineapple in juice (undrained—1 8 oz. can)
- Graham cracker crumbs (1.25 c.)
- Rum extract or rum (0.25 c.)
- Sugar (1 Tbsp.)
- Toasted flaked coconut (0.25 c.)
- Vanilla low-fat, no-sugar ice cream (4 c.)

Instructions

1. Prepare oven to 350 F.
2. Combine butter, cracker crumbs, and sugar. Press into a 2-quart baking dish. Bake 10 minutes and allow to cool completely
3. Combine ice cream, pineapple and juice, and extracts into a bowl with a mixer until well combined. Spread it out into the crust.
4. Freeze for 6 hours.
5. Serve after letting thaw for 5 minutes and topping with coconut shreds.

Kiwi Sorbet

Ingredients

- Kiwi (1 lb., peeled and frozen)
- Honey (0.25 c.)

Instructions

1. Combine everything well in a food processor until mixed.
2. Pour it into a loaf pan and smooth it out.
3. Allow it to freeze for 2 hours. Keep it covered if leaving it overnight in the freezer.

Ricotta Brûlée

Ingredients

- Ricotta cheese (2 c.)
- Lemon zest (1 tsp)
- Honey (2 Tbsp.)
- Sugar (2 Tbsp.)

Instructions

1. Mix together your ricotta, lemon zest, and honey. Then, split into ramekins. Top with sugar and place onto baking sheet.
2. Place oven rack at the topmost position then set the baking sheet in with the broiler on its highest setting. Watch closely and broil until it bubbles and turns golden brown—between 5 and 10 minutes.
3. Cool for 10 minutes and top with any fruits or toppings you prefer.

Chapter 4: Heart-Healthy Gourmet Meals

Grilled Halibut With Pine Nut Relish

Ingredients

- Diced red tomato (0.5 c.)
- Diced yellow tomato (o.5 c)
- EVOO (3 Tbsp.)
- Flour to coat fish
- Green olives (0.5 c.)
- Halibut fillet (4, 1 inch thick)
- Kalamata olives (0.5 c.)
- Lemon juice (1 Tbsp.)
- Zest from a lemon (0.5 tsp.)
- Parsley (2 Tbsp.)
- Pepper to taste
- Pine nuts (3 Tbsp.)
- Salt (pinch to taste)
- Shallot (1)

Instructions

1. Start with toasting the pine nuts in a dry skillet for a few minutes until toasted. Set aside.
2. Combine your tomatoes, the sliced olives, shallot, the lemon juice and zest, and 1 Tbsp. of oil. Mix well and add in parsley and a sprinkle of pepper.
3. Flour fillets, shaking off excess. Season lightly with salt and pepper. Toss the rest of your oil into your skillet and use that to cook the fish until done, flipping halfway over.
4. Serve with relish on top and garnish with pine nuts.

Shrimp Bowls

Ingredients

- Avocado (1, cut small)
- Broccoli (1 lb., florets)
- Ginger (1 Tbsp.)
- Olive oil (2 Tbsp.)
- Plum tomatoes (8 oz., seeds removed and cut)
- Quinoa (1.5 c.)
- Rice vinegar (1 Tbsp.)
- Salt and pepper to taste
- Scallions (2, thinly sliced)
- Shrimp (20 large, peeled and deveined)

Instructions

1. Warm oven to 425 F. Prepare medium saucepan at medium heat and cook the quinoa until toasted, roughly 5 minutes. Add in water (3 c.), then cover immediately. Allow it to cook just below a boil for 10 minutes, then take it off the burner and let it sit for another ten minutes.

2. On a baking sheet, add broccoli, 1 Tbsp. oil, salt, and pepper. Prepare in a single layer. Roast for 15 minutes. Season shrimp, then cook for 6-8 minutes, tossed with broccoli.

3. Mix vinegar, ginger, and remaining oil into a small bowl. Toss with tomatoes and scallions.

4. Serve with quinoa in bowls, topped with broccoli shrimp, then avocado. Finally, add the vinaigrette to the top.

Grilled Watermelon Steak Salad

Ingredients

- Cherry tomatoes (1 lb., halved)
- Honey (1 tsp)
- Lemon juice (3 Tbsp.)
- Mint leaves (1 c., torn up)
- Olive oil (2 Tbsp.)
- Onion (0.5 tsp., small red)
- Parsley (1 c., chopped)
- Salt and pepper
- Sirloin steak (1 lb.)
- Unsalted peanuts to garnish
- Watermelon (3 lbs., seedless)

Instructions

1. Prepare grill to medium-high. Season steak, then grill until done to preference. Allow it to rest on a cutting board.
2. Mix oil, lemon juice, honey, and seasonings. Incorporate the onions and tomatoes as well, folding in nicely.
3. Cut watermelon into 0.5-inch thick triangles and remove rinds. Oil and grill until starting to char—a minute per side, then set aside.
4. Mix the herbs into the tomato mixture. Serve with watermelon topped with stead.

Crispy Cod and Green Beans

Ingredients

- Green Beans (1 lb.)
- Olive oil (2 Tbsp.)
- Parmesan cheese (0.25 c., grated)
- Pepper to taste
- Pesto (2 Tbsp.)
- Salt to taste
- Skinless cod (1.25 lb., four pieces)

Instructions

1. Set oven to 425 F. Put beans onto rimmed baking sheet and combine with 1 Tbsp. oil, then top with cheese and a sprinkling of seasonings. Roast for 10-12 minutes, waiting for it to finally start to brown.

2. Heat remaining oil in a skillet. Season cod and cook until golden brown. You want to use a medium-high heat to do this.

3. Serve with pesto over cod, next to a bed of green beans.

Pistachio-Crusted Fish

Ingredients

- Baby spinach (4 c.)

- Greek yogurt (4 Tbsp.)

- Lemon juice (2 Tbsp.)

- Olive oil (2 Tbsp.)

- Panko (whole-wheat, 0.25 c.)

- Pepper (0.5 tsp)

- Quinoa (0.75 c.)

- Salt (0.75 tsp)

- Shelled pistachios, chopped (0.25 c.)

- Tilapia (4 6-oz. pieces)

Instructions

1. Prepare quinoa based on instructions on packaging.

2. Season fish with salt, pepper, and coat with 1 Tbsp. each of Greek yogurt.

3. Combine panko and pistachios, tossing with 1 Tbsp. olive oil. Gently sprinkle over the top of the fish, pressing it to stick. Bake for 12 minutes at 375 F., or until done.

4. Combine cooked quinoa with spinach, lemon juice, remaining oil, and a pinch of salt and pepper. Serve with fish.

Cumin-Spiced Lamb and Salad

Ingredients

- Carrots (1 lb.)
- Cumin (1.25 tsp.)
- Honey (0.5 tsp.)
- Lamb loin chops (8—about 2 lbs.)
- Mint leaves (0.25 c., fresh)
- Olive oil (3 Tbsp.)
- Radishes (6)
- Red wine vinegar (2 Tbsp.)
- Salt and pepper to taste

Instructions

1. Combine 2 Tbsp. oil, vinegar, a pinch of cumin, honey, and salt and pepper.
2. Warm remaining oil in a skillet at medium. Season lamb with cumin and a pinch of salt and pepper. Cook until preferred doneness.
3. Shave carrots into pieces and create thinly sliced radishes. Coat with dressing and mix with mint. Serve with lamb.

Chapter 5: Heart-Healthy Quick 'n Easy Meals

Sugar Snap Pea and Radish Salad

Ingredients

- Apple-cider vinegar (2 Tbsp.)
- Avocado (0.5, medium ripe)
- Dijon mustard (0.5 tsp)
- Fresh lemon juice (1 Tbsp.)

- Freshly ground pepper (0.5 tsp)
- Ground coriander (0.25 tsp)
- Olive oil (0.25 c.)
- Radishes (12, small)
- Salt (o.5 tsp)
- Sugar snap peas (1 lb.)
- Watermelon radish (1, small)

Instructions

1. Combine peas and radishes in a bowl together.
2. In a blender, combine everything else and puree until well combined and smooth. Add water if necessary to thin it out.
3. Coat radish and peas with dressing and serve.

Horseradish Salmon Cakes

Ingredients

- Dijon mustard (1 Tbsp.)
- English cucumber (1, small)
- Greek Yogurt (2 Tbsp.)
- Horseradish (2 Tbsp.)
- Lemon juice (1 Tbsp.)
- Olive oil (2 Tbsp.)
- Panko (0.25 c.)
- Salt and pepper to taste
- Skinless salmon filet (1.25 lb.)
- Watercress (1 bunch)

Instructions

1. Combine salmon, horseradish, salt and pepper, and mustard into a food processor until well chopped. Then, toss in the bread crumbs and combine well.
2. Form 8 patties.
3. Warm 1 Tbsp. oil in a skillet. Cook until opaque throughout, typically 2 minutes before flipping.
4. Combine yogurt, lemon juice, oil, and a sprinkle of salt and pepper. Combine in cucumber slices, then watercress.
5. Serve salmon with salad.

Salmon, Green Beans, and Tomatoes

Ingredients

- Garlic (6 cloves)
- Green beans (1 lb.)
- Grape tomatoes (1 pint)
- Kalamata olives (0.5 c.)
- Anchovy fillets (3)
- Olive oil (2 Tbsp.)
- Kosher salt and pepper to personal preference
- Salmon fillet, skinless

Instructions

1. Prepare oven to 425 F. Put beans, garlic, olive, anchovy, and tomatoes together along with half of the oil and a pinch of pepper. Roast until veggies are tender.

2. Warm the remainder of the oil over a skillet at medium heat. Season salmon, then cook until done. Serve salmon and veggies together.

Broccoli Pesto Fusilli

Ingredients

- Basil leaves (0.5 c.)
- Broccoli florets (12 oz.)
- Fusilli (12 oz.)
- Garlic (2 cloves)
- Lemon zest (1 Tbsp.)
- Olive oil (3 Tbsp.)
- Parmesan cheese to garnish
- Salt to taste
- Sliced almonds to garnish

Instructions

1. Prepare pasta to directions and reserve 0.5 c. of the liquid.
2. Combine broccoli, garlic, and the reserved water in a bowl and cook for five or six minutes, stirring halfway through. Put everything right into a food processor with the liquid. Combine in basil, oil, zest, a pinch of salt, and puree.
3. Put pasta in with pesto. Drizzle in water if necessary. Sprinkle with cheese and nuts if desired. Serve immediately.

Strawberry Spinach Salad

Ingredients

- Baby spinach (3 c.)
- Medium avocado (0.25, diced)
- Red onion (1 Tbsp.)
- Sliced strawberries (0.5 c.)
- Vinaigrette of choice (2 Tbsp.)
- Walnut pieces (roasted)

Instructions

1. Combine spinach with the berries and onion. Mix well. Coat with vinaigrette and toss. Then, top with walnuts and avocado. Serve.

One-Pot Shrimp and Spinach

Ingredients

- Crushed red pepper (0.25 tsp)
- Garlic (6 cloves, sliced)
- Lemon juice (1 Tbsp.)
- Lemon zest (1.5 tsp.)
- Olive oil (3 Tbsp.)
- Parsley (1 Tbsp.)
- Salt to personal preference
- Shrimp (1 lb.)
- Spinach (1 lb.)

Instructions

1. Warm skillet with 1 Tbsp. oil. Cook half of the garlic until browning, about a single minute. Then, toss in spinach and salt. Wait for it to wilt over the heat, about 5 minutes. Remove and mix in lemon juice, storing it in a separate bowl.
2. Warm heat to medium-high and toss with remainder of oil. Toss in the rest of your garlic and cook until browning. Then, mix in shrimp, pepper, and salt. Cook until shrimp is done, then serve atop spinach with lemon zest and parsley garnish.

Chapter 6: Heart-Healthy Vegetarian and Vegan Meals

Vegetarian Butternut Squash Torte

Ingredients

- Butternut squash (1 lb.)
- Crusty bread of choice
- Kale (1, small)
- Olive oil (1 Tbsp.)
- Parmesan cheese (4 Tbsp., grated)
- Plum tomato (1)
- Provolone cheese (6 oz., thinly sliced)
- Red onion (1, medium)
- Salt and pepper to taste
- Yukon Gold potato (1, medium)

Instructions

1. Take a spring form 9-inch pan and prepare it so that nothing will stick. Then, take your squash and put it around the bottom in circles to sort of mimic a crust.
2. Then, layer it with the onion, with the rings separated out.
3. Add half of your kale, then sprinkle half of your oil, and season to taste.
4. Then, layer with potatoes, half of your cheese, and top with the last of your kale.
5. Add the oil, onion, tomato slices, and the last of your cheese.
6. Top it with the remainder of your squash, then coat with parmesan.
7. Bake, covering the top with foil, for 20 minutes. Then, discard the foil and let it bake until it is tender and browning, typically another ten minutes or so.

Vegetarian Fried Rice

Ingredients

- 2 eggs (leave out if vegan)
- Garlic (2 cloves, pressed)
- Kale (6 oz., thinly sliced leaves)
- Olive oil (1 Tbsp.)
- Rice (4 c., cooked and chilled, preferably the day before)
- Sesame oil (1 Tbsp.)
- Shiitake mushroom caps (4 oz., sliced)
- Soy sauce (2 Tbsp., low sodium)
- Sriracha (1 tsp.)

Instructions

1. Start by warming your oil up in your pan of choice or wok. Your oil should be just before the smoking point.
2. Cook the mushrooms and toss until they start to turn golden brown, usually just a few minutes, then set them off for later.
3. Toss in some sesame oil and kale, cooking until wilted, then add in your garlic as well for another minute.
4. Take your rice and mix it in as well, tossing it together until heated.
5. Move all rice to the side, then pour beaten eggs in the center of your pan. Stir often until the eggs are just about finished, and then mix into the rice.
6. Mix in the soy sauce and sriracha, then top with mushrooms.

Vegan Butternut Squash Soup

Ingredients

- Butternut squash (1, 2.5 lbs. with skin and seeds removed—keep seeds)

- Carrots (2 medium, cut into 1-inch pieces)

- Coconut milk (2 Tbsp.)

- Olive oil (2 Tbsp., and one tsp)

- Onion (1, large, chopped)

- Pepper (2.25 tsp)

- Turmeric (2.25 tsp)

- Veggie bouillon base (1 Tbsp.)

Instructions

1. Take a Dutch oven and add 2 Tbsp. oil. Warm, then cook your onions until soft and translucent, roughly 6 minutes or so.

2. Integrate your bouillon base with 6 c., boiling water until completely dissolved.

3. Toss together your veggies, turmeric, and pepper into your onions in the Dutch oven. Allow it to cook for a minute before mixing in your veggie broth. Simmer for 20 minutes until veggies are soft.

4. Turn your oven to 375F. Take your seeds and your oil that is remaining and combine them together. Then, coat it up with the turmeric and pepper before toasting in your oven for about 1o minutes.

5. With a blender or immersion blender, combine your soup until smooth.

6. Serve topped with seeds and a swirl of coconut milk.

Vegetarian Kale and Sweet Potato Frittata

Ingredients

- Eggs (6)
- Garlic (2 cloves)
- Goat cheese (3 oz.)
- Half-and-half (1 c.)
- Kale (2 c., packed tightly)
- Olive oil (2 Tbsp.)
- Pepper (0.5 tsp.)
- Red onion (0.5, small)
- Salt (1 tsp.)
- Sweet potatoes (2 c.)

Instructions

1. With your oven warming, combine your eggs in a bowl. Then, add in the salt and half-and-half as well. Make sure your oven is at 350F.

2. In a nonstick skillet that you can put into your oven, cook your potatoes over 1 Tbsp. of oil. Wait for them to soften and start to turn golden. Then, remove from the pan.

3. Next, cook your kale, onion, and garlic together in the remainder of your oil until it is wilted and aromatic.

4. Put your potato back in with the kale, then pour your egg mix atop it all. Incorporate well and then allow it to cook on the stove for another 3 minutes.

5. Top it all with the goat cheese, then bake for 10 minutes until completely done.

Vegan Ginger Ramen

Ingredients

- Garlic (4 cloves, minced)
- Ginger (0.33 c., chopped coarsely)
- Grapeseed oil (0.5 c.)
- Low-sodium soy sauce (2 Tbsp.)
- Pepper (1 tsp., freshly ground)
- Ramen noodles (*real,* fresh noodles—not the $0.10 packaged stuff)
- Rice vinegar (1 Tbsp.)
- Salt to personal preference
- Scallions (1 bunch—about 2 c. sliced)
- Sesame oil (1 tsp)
- Sugar (0.5 tsp)

Instructions

1. Combine your ginger with the minced garlic and roughly 60% of your scallions.
2. Warm up the grapeseed oil until just before the smoking point. Then, take the oil and dump it over your scallion mix. It will sizzle and wilt, turning green. Leave it for 5 minutes, then add in the rest of the scallions.
3. Carefully combine in soy sauce, sesame oil, vinegar, sugar, and pepper, and leave it to incorporate for the next 15 minutes or so. Adjust flavor accordingly.
4. Prepare your noodles to the package instructions. Drain.
5. Introduce your noodles to your scallion sauce and coat well.
6. Serve topped with sesame seeds or any other toppings you may want.

Vegan Glazed Tofu
Ingredients

- Canola oil (0.5 c.)
- Firm tofu (12 oz.)
- Ginger (0.5" sliced thinly)
- Maple syrup (3 Tbsp.—you can use honey if you're not vegan.)
- Pepper flakes (0.5 tsp.)
- Rice vinegar (3 Tbsp.)
- Soy sauce (4 Tbsp.)
- Toppings of choice—recommended ones include rice, scallions, or sesame seeds

Instructions

1. Dry and drain your tofu out, squeezing it between paper towels so that you can remove as much of the liquid as you possibly can, then slice it into cubes.
2. Combine the wet ingredients together, and add in your pepper and ginger.
3. Warm your wok or skillet. When the oil is shimmery, gingerly place your tofu into it carefully and leave it for around 4 minutes so that it can brown. It should be dark brown when you flip. Repeat on both sides. Then, drop the heat down and toss in your sauce mix. Allow it to reduce until it is thick, roughly 4 minutes.
4. Put tofu on plates and top with anything you desire.

Vegan Greek Tofu Breakfast Scramble

Ingredients

- Basil (0.25 c., chopped)
- Firm tofu block (8 oz.)
- Garlic (2 cloves, diced)
- Grape tomatoes (0.5 c., halved)
- Kalamata olives (0.25 c., halved)
- Lemon juice (from ½ lemon)
- Nutritional yeast (2 Tbsp.)
- Olive oil (1 Tbsp.)
- Red bell pepper (0.5 c., chopped)
- Red onion (0.25, diced)
- Salt (pinch)
- Spinach (1 handful)
- Tahini paste (1 tsp)
- Salt and pepper to personal preference

Instructions

1. Break down tofu until the shape/texture of scrambled eggs. Then, combine in yeast, lemon juice, and tahini. Sprinkle with a pinch of salt.
2. Prepare skillet at a moderate heat. Sauté onions for 5 minutes before tossing in the pepper and garlic for an additional 5 minutes.
3. Mix in tofu and Kalamata olives. Warm through.
4. Toss in greens until wilted and reduced. Take off from heat and toss in tomatoes and season with salt and pepper to taste.

PART IV

What is Plant-Based Eating? How Does It Differ From Veganism?
What are The Health Benefits of Eating Plant-Based Food?

When people hear the words, "plant-based eating," they usually assume they would need to sacrifice good food for healthy living… this is not the case. Not only do you feel great when you make the switch, but you will find the food to be delicious and quite filling. Being plant-based is not about just eating salad. Salad will be very boring… probably after the second one. There is not a single person on earth who will like salad that much. There are so many different varieties of foods to eat, you just need to be creative, and sort of learn how to cook. So, what is a plant-based diet, you ask? This is a diet that consists of the consumption of whole grains, fruits, vegetables, nuts, legumes, and beans. You will eat a lot of different varieties of rice and potatoes if you are not concerned about carb-intake.

Which brings me to discuss the difference between veganism and a plant-based diet: Veganism is defined as the rejection of all animal products and animal by-products to further prevent the exploitation and suffering of animals. It is a lifestyle that is not just a diet, it includes the rejection of clothing, shoe, household product, and make-up companies that profit or participate in the maltreatment of animal. The products they purchase are frequently stamped with an encircled "V" with the sub-title "cruelty-free" underneath it. This differs greatly from simply being plant-based… this lifestyle is not usually based on the welfare of animals.

Plant-based lifestyle usually pertains to a healthy lifestyle that includes being active and only eating foods that originate from plants. Even though "veganism" and "plant-based" are often interchangeable terms and most people do not know the difference. A plant-based eater is specifically concerned for their health and how they can better it.

The benefits of going plant-based range from a healthy, glowing complexion to reducing the risk of developing cancer. According to Dr. David Katz, a practicing physician, and researcher at Yale Universities Prevention and Research Center, "A diet of minimally processed foods close to nature, predominantly plants, is decisively associated with health promotion and disease prevention." Plant-based diets are a surefire way to make sure you get all your vitamins and nutrients. If you plan your meals out properly and are willing to try the same foods in a new way, there's no reason why you should be vitamin-deficient (DISCLAIMER: This is not including chronic health problem where you have difficulties absorbing certain vitamins)

When you try to consume more wholesome foods like fruits, vegetables, whole grains, other complex carbohydrates, beans, legumes, nuts, seeds, and lots of water, you are allowing yourself fewer health problems. You are more likely to lose unnecessary weight, and you will have a significantly lower risk of heart disease. Eating less meat will reduce your risk of stroke, cardiovascular problems, and diabetes. Your blood pressure will be more regulated due to regular consumption of whole grains, Omega fatty acids, potassium, and less intake of sodium.

You will be able to manage your blood sugar by regularly consuming foods high in fiber. Fiber slows down the absorption of sugars in your bloodstream and keeps you full longer. Fiber-dense foods balance out your cortisol levels, which in turn will make you less stressed out. Also, when you switch to plant-based food, you will reduce your risk of developing cancer, like breast or colon. Inflammation may also subside; if you have arthritis, studies show that when you cut out dairy and meat from your diet, your arthritic symptoms can improve and reduce flare-ups. There are almost too many benefits to count, and way too many to list. The only way to see the broad spectrum of these benefits is to see for yourself.

Chapter Two:

Clinical Studies: Science-Backed Proof

A 2011 study[123] from Canada found 62.1% of Canadians to be overweight and

25.4% of the population to be obese. This study found vegans and vegetarians,

regardless of gender, age, or location, to make up less than 6% of the

obese/overweight population. Did you know that dietary cholesterol only

comes from meat, fish, eggs, and milk? The same study found vegans to have

significantly lower levels of cholesterol in their blood... which means a plant-

based diet will not put you at risk to have clogged arteries or heart disease.

Type 2 diabetes and cancer are both prevalent diseases of people who regularly

consume animal products.

---

[1] Public Health Agency of Canada [website] Obesity in Canada: prevalence among adults. Ottawa, ON: Public Health Agency of Canada; 2011. Available from: www.phac-aspc.gc.ca/hp-ps/hl-mvs/oic-oac/adult-eng.php. Accessed 2018 May 14.
From <https://www.ncbi.nlm.nih.gov/pmc/articles/PMC5638464/>

[2] Statistics Canada [website] Body mass index of Canadian children and youth, 2009 to 2011. Ottawa, ON: Statistics Canada; 2013. Available from: www.statcan.gc.ca/pub/82-625-x/2012001/article/11712-eng.htm. Accessed 2018 May 12
From <https://www.ncbi.nlm.nih.gov/pmc/articles/PMC5638464/>

[3] Statistics Canada [website] Body composition of Canadian adults, 2009 to 2011. Ottawa, ON: Statistics Canada; 2013. Available from: www.statcan.gc.ca/pub/82-625-x/2012001/article/11708-eng.htm. Accessed 2018 May 12.
From <https://www.ncbi.nlm.nih.gov/pmc/articles/PMC5638464/>

In 2015, the World Health Organization (W. H. O.) found evidence[4] linking

red and processed meat consumption to colorectal cancer. This study has also

found overwhelming evidence to classify processed meats such as sausages,

bacon, ham, beef jerky, corned beef, smoked, fermented, and cured meats, as a

group 1 carcinogen. The Academy of Nutrition and Dietetics stated that a

vegan diet (when properly planned) could provide the prevention and treatment

of many diseases and ailments-- it can be perfect for any person in any stage of

life, including pregnancy, infancy, and athletic.

Aside from how animal products affect our health, maintenance of livestock has

quite a negative impact on the Earth as well. The consumption of animal

products uses an astonishing and disturbing amount of earthly resources. 60

Billion animals, per annum, are used to feed the human population. Livestock

production is responsible for 18 % of the greenhouse gas emissions. That is

more than all the vehicles on earth emit into the ozone layer. To produce a

kilogram (2.2 pounds) of beef, it requires seventy times the amount of land

required to produce the same amount of weight in vegetables. The amount of

[4] World Health Organization [website] Carcinogenicity of consumption of red processed meat Lancet. Oncol. 2015 Dec; 16(16):1599-600.

all irrigation water[5] , the amount that is used to produce livestock is calculated to increase from 15% to 50% by 2025.

Another study[6] on people with rheumatoid arthritis, published in the journal of the American Dietetic Association in 2010, stated that when you switch to a plant-based diet, you will reduce your joint inflammation. There were significant improvements in joint tenderness, duration of stiffness in the morning, and better grip strength. Vitamins B-12 and D, Calcium, and Essential Fatty-Acids are essential for bone health. Fatty Acids are commonly found in olive and canola oils, chia, flax, and hemp seeds.

A study[7] from Massachusetts General Hospital associates high consumption levels of animal protein in the human diet with higher mortality rates. The longest study of the effects of different sources of proteins, like processed and even unprocessed red meats versus plant-based, found trends in plant-based proteins and lower risk of mortality. There is a suggestion to replace some proteins with carbohydrates—which produces some health benefits, like weight management, reduced blood pressure, and other

---

[5] A global assessment of the water footprint of farm animal products. 2012;15(3): 401-15. Epub 2012 Jan 24.

[6] A study done on vegan and vegetarian diets about joint health, *Journal of the American Dietetic Association, 2010.*
From < https://www.arthritis.org/living-with-arthritis/arthritis-diet/anti-inflammatory/vegan-and-vegetarian-diets.php>

[7] Edward Giovannucci et al. **Association of Animal and Plant Protein Intake With All-Cause and Cause-Specific Mortality**. *JAMA Internal Medicine*, 2016 DOI: 10.1001/jamainternmed.2016.4182

cardiovascular issues. This study stated that consuming more plant-sourced protein will help you have healthier well-being.

Apparently, going plant-based will save trillions of dollars, millions of lives, and very possibly the Earth. A study[8] done at Oxford University compared three scenarios pertaining to veganism: Researchers compared the effects of veganism and global mortality rates, greenhouse gas emissions, and health from an economic standpoint. A world-wide adoption of a plant-based diet predicted to prevent 8.1 million deaths per annum and reduce deaths from all causes by 10% by 2050. Adopting a plant-based diet will reduce food-related greenhouse gases by 70% by 2050.

Also, going plant-based is projected to save $1067 billion USD a year in costs related to health care. Going plant-based could literally save the world. This study is basically saying that the consumption of animal products causes an obscene amount of health problems.

---

[8] Analysis and valuation of the health and climate change cobenefits of dietary change

Marco Springmann, H. Charles J. Godfray, Mike Rayner, and Peter Scarborough

PNAS April 12, 2016. 113 (15) 4146-4151; published ahead of print March 21, 2016.

https://doi.org/10.1073/pnas.1523119113

Chapter Three:

Basic Four-Week Meal Plan

(also, an explanation of some vital vitamins)

(The following meal plan is not designed for weight loss or to build muscle. It is not a low-fat meal plan although you may take out or add any of the ingredients as you see fit. This is not a low-carb meal plan, you can always add more produce. Also, this is not a super-high protein plan meant for pregnant women or athletes. If you are either of these, I suggest adding more protein.)

Breakfast is absolutely the most important meal of the day. You fast for about eight hours while you sleep and when you wake up your blood sugar will be low. Even though you may not be hungry, it is important to get a little something in your stomach for fuel for your body. Your first meal should consist of protein-dense, high-fiber ingredients. These two will help keep you full and energized for the day ahead. Eating five or six small meals throughout the day will give you the boosts you need to not crash hallway through your workload. Drinking lots of water is equally important. Sometimes dehydration will mask itself as hunger.

There are a few nutrients and vitamins that will most likely come up in conversation a lot as a plant-based eater; These include vitamin D, Iron, Protein, and B12.

Vitamin D: Required to be able to absorb calcium properly. Ultimately, the best way to get Vitamin D into your system is through sunlight. Every living thing needs sunlight since it is vital for life to exist. It only takes about five to thirty minutes of sunlight twice a week for us to be able to get all the Vitamin D we need. Many plant-based milks and cereals are fortified with vitamin D. Mushrooms are naturally loaded with vitamin D. The best way to get vitamin D is by going outside and soaking up some sun. A plus side to this is the sun keeps depression at bay.

B-12: When it comes to a plant-based diet, B-12 is hard to come by in food...naturally. It is in soil, and I also produced by the bacteria in your gut, so unless you do not want to wash your produce, the best way to get your B-12 is probably through a daily supplement. Since the oral bioavailability is relatively low, try to find one with a relatively high level of a daily value percentage.

Five sources of B12 include:

1. Most plant-based milks are fortified with B12

2. The same goes for most cereals

3. Plant-based butter spreads

4. Nutritional yeast

5. Nori (seaweed)

Protein: The recommended amount of protein for the average woman is approximately 52 grams per day and for the average man, 63 grams per day. There is protein in almost everything a plant-based eater regularly consumes. Despite the controversy, protein is one of the most easily obtainable of the nutrients. Vegetables, fruits, beans, whole grains, legumes, nuts, and seeds sometimes have just some, and others have quite a bit of protein. The typical American diet has almost too much protein. Unless you are pregnant or athletic, you really do not need as much protein as you would think. Diets high in protein tend to increase chances of osteoporosis and kidney disease.

The top 12 food that contains the highest levels of protein are:
1. Black Beans
2. Tofu
3. Nuts
4. Tempeh
5. Chickpeas
6. Broccoli
7. Quinoa
8. Lentils
9. Potatoes
10. Mushrooms
11. Plant-based milk
12. Plant-based yogurt

Iron: Even though iron is the most common nutrient to be deficient in human. When you are a plant-eater, getting plenty of iron into your system is easier than you would imagine. If you pair it with some form of vitamin C, you will not have any problems with anemia; Vitamin C helps your body absorb iron.

Here are the top ten sources of iron:
1. Tomato Paste
2. White Beans
3. Cooked Soybeans
4. Lentils
5. Dried Apricots
6. Spirulina

7. Spinach
8. Quinoa
9. Blackstrap Molasses
10. Prune Juice

Here is a basic Four-Week Meal Plan with recipes from all different sources. If you are not sure of how to make the recipe, there are many different variations from Minimalist Baker, Forks Over Knives, YouTube, or Eat This Much online. It is relatively simple to follow, and there is no right way to go about this plan.

WEEK 1	Breakfast	Snack	Lunch	Snack	Dinner
Monday	Oatmeal with raspberries blueberries chia seeds cinnamon almonds	Blue-Corn Chips, Black Bean Hummus	Jambalaya with Bell Peppers, Chickpeas	Fresh Fruit	Soup: Potatoes, onions, carrots, veggie broth, bay leaf, olive oil, salt, and pepper
Tuesday	Bananas with plant milk and cinnamon	Fruit, Mixed Nuts	Peanut Butter, Banana and Chia seed sandwich	Apple and Broccoli salad with Olive oil, Lemon juice, Salt, and peppercorn dressing	Rice and Black Bean burrito. Add tomatoes, spinach, salsa, avocado.
Wednesday	Oatmeal	Pretzels, carrots, celery, and peanut butter	Spaghetti with Pasta Sauce of your choice	Pretzels and Orange Juice	Quinoa Stuffed Bell Peppers
Thursday	Coconut yogurt with granola	Chips with Hummus	Whole Wheat bagel with almond butter and Banana	Apple and Broccoli Salad	Black Bean Burgers
Friday	Smoothie: Banana, Spinach, blueberries, Hemp Seeds	Pretzels and Orange	Whole wheat toast with cacao and almond butter spread with Berries	Mixed nuts and fruit	Rice and Veggie soup

Saturday	Oatmeal	Chia, Banana, Almond Butter Wrap	Jambalaya with chickpeas and steamed veggies	Pretzels and Orange	Spaghetti
Sunday	Yogurt and granola	Hummus and chips	Peanut Butter and Jelly Sandwich with fruit	Fresh fruit and steamed veggies	Burritos with Walnut Meat

WEEK 2	Breakfast	Snack	Lunch	Snack	Dinner
Monday	Oatmeal	Apples and peanut butter	Pad Thai	Fresh fruit	Mixed Veggies with Brown Rice and Soy Sauce
Tuesday	Cinnamon Apple Toast	Strawberries and Chocolate Almond Milk	Tomato Soup with whole wheat garlic toast	Fresh fruit and veggies	Steamed Veggies with brown rice and sweet potato fries
Wednesday	Banana Oatmeal Smoothie	Peanut Butter and Celery	Fully Loaded Salad with Balsamic Dressing	Peanut Butter and carrots	Garlic, White wine pasta with Brussel sprouts
Thursday	Granola and coconut yogurt	Fruit and Mixed nuts	Fully loaded burrito	Chocolate Banana Smoothie	Pad Thai
Friday	Overnight Oats	Strawberries and chocolate almond milk	Couscous with pine nuts and bell peppers	Tomato and hummus on rye bread	Mixed veggies with brown rice and soy sauce
Saturday	Banana Almond Butter Toast	Pretzels and Orange	Pad Thai	Mixed Nuts	Spaghetti with Spiralized Zucchini
Sunday	Overnight Oats	Yogurt and Granola	Peanut Butter and Jelly sandwich	Pretzels and Orange	Burritos

WEEK 3	Breakfast	Snack	Lunch	Snack	Dinner
Monday	Banana Oatmeal Smoothie	Spinach Salad with Carrots	Kale and Avocado Salad	Cantaloupe with granola	White Spaghetti
Tuesday	High Protein Smoothie with Granola	Peanut Butter and Celery	Avocado Pasta Sauce	Spinach and Tomato Salad	Zucchini Peanut Noodles
Wednesday	Overnight Oatmeal	Spinach and Tomato Salad	Apricot Jam and Almond Butter Sandwich	Cabbage and Carrot Juice with Granola	Sea Salt Edamame and Lemon Cous-Cous salad
Thursday	Raspberry Chia Seed Pudding and Oranges	Basic Green smoothie with Red Bell Peppers	Banana, Peanut Butter, and Raisins with Peanut Butter and Celery	Mixed Nuts	White Spaghetti
Friday	Oatmeal and Apples with Granola	Celery and Hummus	Hummus Pocket Sandwich	Sliced Cucumber and Avocado	Fresh Tomato Pasta, Green beans with olive oil
Saturday	Chocolate milk with oatmeal, raisins, and dates	Cantaloupe and Red Pepper and Hummus	Carrot, Hummus, and avocado	Peanut Butter and Celery	Burritos

Sunday	Blueberry, Almond Butter protein smoothie	Peanut Butter and Celery	Avocado Pasta Sauce	Cucumber and Tomato toss with Granola	Sweet Potato noodles, Cashew Sauce and Brussel Sprouts

WEEK 4	Breakfast	Snack	Lunch	Snack	Dinner
Monday	Oatmeal with raspberries blueberries chia seeds cinnamon almonds	Blue-Corn Chips, Black Bean Hummus	Jambalaya with Bell Peppers, Chickpeas	Fresh Fruit	Soup: Potatoes, onions, carrots, veggie broth, bay leaf, olive oil, salt, and pepper
Tuesday	Bananas with plant milk and cinnamon	Fruit, Mixed Nuts	Peanut Butter, Banana and Chia seed sandwich	Apple and Broccoli salad with Olive oil, Lemon juice, Salt, and peppercorn dressing	Rice and Black Bean burrito. Add tomatoes, spinach, salsa, avocado.
Wednesday	Oatmeal	Pretzels, carrots, celery, and peanut butter	Spaghetti with Pasta Sauce of your choice	Pretzels and Orange Juice	Quinoa Stuffed Bell Peppers
Thursday	Coconut yogurt with granola	Chips with Hummus	Whole Wheat bagel with almond butter and Banana	Apple and Broccoli Salad	Black Bean Burgers
Friday	Smoothie: Banana, Spinach, blueberries, Hemp Seeds	Pretzels and Orange	Whole wheat toast with cacao and	Mixed nuts and fruit	Rice and Veggie soup

			almond butter spread with Berries		
Saturday	Oatmeal	Chia, Banana, Almond Butter Wrap	Jambalaya, chickpeas, steamed veggies	Pretzels and Orange	Spaghetti
Sunday	Yogurt and granola	Hummus and chips	Peanut Butter and Jelly Sandwich with fruit	Fresh fruit and steamed veggies	Burritos with Walnut Meat

PART V

UNDERSTAND THE RESISTANCE

There are times when our cells quit responding to our insulin. When this happens, you are likely suffering from insulin resistance. Your cells become resistant to insulin. When your body becomes resistant, your pancreas will respond by producing more insulin to try and reduce your blood sugar levels. When this happens you develop hyperinsulinemia, which is when the blood contains high levels of insulin. Let's make this a little easier, let's look at the separate parts of insulin resistance.

Metabolism

Metabolism is probably one of the most misunderstood processes that the body goes through. Your metabolism works as a collection of chemical reactions that happens in your cells to help you convert food into energy. As you are reading this, a thousand metabolic reactions are happening. There are two main metabolic channels.

- Catabolism is the process your body goes through when breaking down you food components, as in fats, proteins, and carbs, into simpler parts, which are then used for energy. To better understand it, look at it as if it is your destructive metabolism. Your cells break down fats and carbs to release their energy; this ensures that your body can fuel an anabolic reaction.

- Anabolism is the contrastive metabolism which works to build and store energy. When your cells perform an anabolic process, it helps to grow new cells and to maintain your body tissues, and it also helps to store energy that you can use later.

The nervous and hormone systems control these processes. When you look at how many calories you should consume in a day, you have to check your body's total energy expenditure. What you eat, how much you move, how you rest, and how well your tissues and cells recuperate will all go into figuring out your total energy expenditure.

Your metabolism is made up of three main components:

1. Basal metabolic rate – this how many calories you body can burn while at rest, and also contributes to 50 to 80 percent of the amount of energy you body uses.
2. How much energy is used during activity – this is how many calories your body burns when you are active. This takes up 20% of your total expenditure.
3. Warming effects of your food – this is how many calories you use when you eat, digest, and metabolize your food.

Insulin

Insulin is a hormone that the pancreas produces and releases into your blood. Insulin helps to keep your blood sugar at a reasonable level by promoting cell growth and division, protein and lipid metabolism, regulating carbohydrates, and glucose uptake. Insulin helps your cells absorb glucose to use for energy.

After you eat, and your blood sugar levels rise, insulin is released. The glucose and insulin travel throughout your blood to your cells. It helps to stimulate the muscle tissue and liver; helps liver, fat, and muscle cells to absorb glucose; and lowers glucose levels by reducing the glucose production in your liver.

People who suffer from type 1 or type 2 diabetes may have to take insulin shot to help their bodies metabolize glucose correctly. Type 1 diabetic's pancreas doesn't make insulin, and the beta cells have been destroyed. There's typically no chance of preventing type 1, and most of the time a person is born with it. Type 2 diabetic's pancreas still makes insulin, but the body doesn't respond to it.

Symptoms

If you go to the doctor, they will likely test your fasting insulin levels. If you have high levels, then chances are you are insulin resistant. You can also do an oral glucose tolerance test. This is where you will be given a dose of glucose, and they will check your blood sugar levels for the next few hours.

People who are obese or overweight, and people with a lot of fat in the mid-section, are at a greater risk of being insulin resistant. Acanthosis nigrans, a skin condition characterized by dark spots on the skin, can be a symptom of insulin resistance. Also, if you have low HDL and high triglycerides, then your chances are higher as well.

For the most part, insulin resistance and pre-diabetes have no significant symptoms. They main way to find out if you have either one is to get tested by your doctor. Now, you're probably wondering how to know if you should be tested. Here are some reasons why you should:

- Body Mass Index over 25
- Over age 45
- Have CVD
- Physically inactive
- Parent or sibling with diabetes
- Family background of Pacific Islander American, Hispanic/Latino, Asian American, Native American, Alaska Native, or African American
- Had a baby that weighed more than 9 pounds
- Diagnoses of gestational diabetes
- High blood pressure – 140/90 or higher
- HDL below 35 or triglyceride above 250
- Have polycystic ovary syndrome

If your tests come back as normal, be sure to be retested every three years, at least. But, you don't have to wait until you get positive test results to start changing your life. In fact, if you have any of the risk factors, even if it's just a family history, you start changing now, and you may never have to hear that diagnoses.

INSULIN RESISTANCE DIET

Years of research has found that excess weight is the primary cause of insulin resistance. This means that weight loss can help your body better respond to insulin. Studies performed by the Diabetes Prevention Program have found that people who are pre-diabetic and insulin resistance can prevent or slow down the development of diabetes by fixing their diet.

Guidelines

Here are the main seven ways you go start to develop an insulin resistance diet:

1. Reduce Carbohydrate Intake

Studies that have been published in *Diabetes, Metabolic Syndrome and Obesity* suggest that controlling the number of carbohydrates you eat is essential in controlling your glycemic index. You can count all carbs you eat, but it's best if you make sure you consume your carbs from dairy products, legumes, whole grains, fruits, and veggies.

2. Stay Away From Sweetened Beverages

All sugars will raise your blood sugar levels, but the American Diabetes Association has now advised, specifically, to avoid sugar-sweetened drinks. This includes iced tea, fruit drinks, soft drinks, and vitamin or energy water drinks that have artificial sweeteners, concentrates, high fructose corn syrup, or sucrose.

3. Consume More Fiber

Glycemia is improved in people who consume more than 50 grams of fiber each day. Large prospective cohort studies have shown that whole grain consumption is associated with a lower risk of type 2 diabetes.

4. Consume Healthy Fats

Studies have shown that fatty acids are more important than total fat. People who suffer from insulin resistance should consume unsaturated fats instead of trans fatty acids or saturated fats.

5. Consume Plenty of Protein

International Journal of Vitamin and Nutrition Research published a study in 2011 that discovered people who were on a diet to treat obesity had better results when they consumed more protein.

6. Consume Dairy

More and more studies are finding that dairy consumption is linked to a reduced risk of type 2 diabetes.

7. Watch Your Portions

Losing weight is key in reducing your risk for diabetes. One great way to do that controls your portion sizes. It's best to eat more small meals instead of three large meals.

Bad Foods

When you start the insulin resistance diet, there are certain foods that you need to avoid, or at least reduce your intake of. Here are some of the foods that you need to watch out for.

- Red meat – contains lots of saturated fats that can exacerbate the problems

- Certain cheeses – cheese that is high in fat will cause more problems

- Fried food – this is a bad dietary choice no matter what diet you're on

- Grains – processed or refined carbs can lead higher insulin levels

- Potatoes – these foods turn into sugar in your system

- Pumpkin – these are just like potatoes

- Carrots – these aren't entirely bad for you, just limit your intake because they are high in sugar

- Doughnuts – these are full insulin raising ingredients

- Alcohol – these turn straight to sugar when you drink them

Good Foods

Now that you know the main foods you should stay away from, here are the foods you should consume.

- Broccoli, Spinach, Collard greens – these, as well as most other leafy greens, are a great source of magnesium, zinc, vitamin E, C, and A

- Broccoli sprouts

- Swiss Chard, Romaine Lettuce, Arugula, Green Cabbage, and Kale – these also contain high amounts of nutrients

- Blueberries – contain anthocyanins which simulate the release of adiponectin which helps regular blood sugar

- Indian gooseberry – these can regulate blood sugar and reduce hyperglycemia

- Walnuts – any nut is great food for an insulin resistance diet

These are just a few of some of the foods you should consume. Many other foods have the same properties as the ones on this list, as well as a few other types of benefits.

LONG-TERM MANAGEMENT

Once you have started a diet, the hardest thing is sticking with it. The good thing about this diet is that it isn't anything drastic, and you can quickly change your diet with a few tweaks. To ensure that you have lasting results, let's look at some of the best ways to maintain.

Be sure to keep up regular exercise. Exercise can help lower your blood sugar, reduce body fat, and help you lose weight. Your cells will also become more insulin sensitive as well. You don't have to do anything spectacular either. Any movement will help you; gardening, running, swimming, walking, or dancing all count for exercise.

Remember that weight loss isn't going to be linear. You may start dropping pounds when you first start, but you will eventually hit a plateau. You have to be proactive with your diet. When you notice you are hitting a plateau, start to make little changes to push past it.

Try to pay attention to when you eat. If you notice that you eat when you are stress, upset, sad, bored, lonely, or low on energy take note of it. Look for other ways to move past those emotions to prevent emotional eating.

Find some cheerleaders. I don't mean paying people to follow you around all day cheering, that would get annoying. I mean you should find a support system. The main reason why diet programs like Jenny Craig and Weight

Watchers works are because of the meeting and people to talk to. There's no need to pay big bucks for this thought. You can get your family and friends to help you out, and you can probably find a Facebook group to help you out.

Side Effects

With any diet, you will experience some side effects. These side effects will either be longer-term or short-term. Let's look at some side effects that you may experience when you begin the insulin resistance diet.

- Short-term:
  - Cravings – this is normal when you start to change your diet. Your body becomes freaked out when you start to eat healthier foods and reduce the snack foods that you're used to eating. Keep reminding yourself why you're doing this. The cravings will eventually pass.
  - Headaches – this is because your body has become addicted to the processed foods you're used to eating. You're going to withdrawals. Once you get all the bad food out of your system, the headaches will stop.
  - Lower energy – this is another symptom you will have because of withdrawals. Your energy levels will drop. Your body is doing a lot of work when you start eating healthier, so be patient with it.

- Long-term:
  - Weight loss – this is probably the best thing that will happen to you on this diet. Weight loss will help to improve all of your health problems.
  - Less hunger and cravings – you may start out having more cravings, but once that phase passes, you won't be bothered with the hunger and cravings like you used to be.
  - Lower blood pressure – a diet that is low in sugar and trans and saturated fats, your blood pressure will lower. This reduces your risk of heart disease, heart attack, stroke, and several other health problems.
  - More energy – getting rid of high glycemic index foods will give bursts of energy that you have never had. Plus, you will no longer have the rollercoaster effect from your blood sugar highs and lows.
  - Better mood and concentration – with your old diet, you probably had mood boosts followed by a sudden plummet. With the insulin resistance diet, you will keep a more steady mood and concentration throughout the day.
  - Better immune system – since you won't be consuming as many inflammatory and allergenic foods you will be able to improve your overall immune system and health.

o Increased digestion – with this diet you will reduce your intake of sugar, dairy, and gluten. These foods are the most common foods to cause digestive problems. Since you won't be consuming as many of these foods, your digestive system will work better. You will also increase your fiber intake, so this will aid your gastrointestinal tract as well.

As you can see, the long-term side effects are better than the short-term side effects; there are also more long-term effects. It's easy to see the good outweighs the bad. It's a no brainer that this is an easy and simple diet to follow.

DIET PLAN

To help get you started, here is a 5-day meal plan. All of the recipes will follow in the next chapter.

<u>Day One</u>

Breakfast: Basil and Tomato Frittata

Frittatas are the perfect breakfast to help use up leftovers. Pair this with a slice of whole grain toast and fruit.

Lunch: Carrot and Butternut Squash Soup

You'll never go back to canned soups after you try this.

Dinner: Grilled Shrimp Skewers

This is a quick meal because shrimp only takes a few minutes to cook.

<u>Day Two</u>

Breakfast: Pecan, Carrot, and Banana Muffins

This is a meal you can serve to your friends, and nobody will ever know that they are healthy. It's the perfect guilt-free treat.

Lunch: Lemony Hummus

Creating your hummus is a great meal. You have control over its flavor and salt levels.

Dinner: Chicken Tortilla Soup

This is perfect if you have some leftover chicken. This spicy soup will satisfy everyone.

Day Three

Breakfast: Dried Fruit, Seeds, and Nuts Granola

This is great to mix up a large amount on the weekend and portion it out for the following week.

There is a high carb content because of the dried fruit, but you can easily fix that by reducing the fruit or leaving it out entirely.

Lunch: Quinoa Tabbouleh Salad

Quinoa is the perfect food because not only is it gluten-free, but it's also considered a protein. This is a delicious meal for meat-eaters and vegetarians.

Dinner: Rice and Beef Stuffed Peppers

These little peppers look sophisticated, but the entire family will love eating them up.

Day Four

Breakfast: Goat Cheese and Veggie Scramble

This is the perfect savory breakfast. With the onions, tomatoes, peppers, eggs, and cheese you have the perfect well-rounded meal.

Lunch: Curried Chicken Salad

The Greek yogurt and mayo adds creaminess to the sandwich that you won't get anywhere else.

Dinner: Jamaican Pork Tenderloin with Beans

This is a quick summertime meal that everybody will love. Serve alongside some pilaf or brown rice.

Day Five

Breakfast: Superfood Smoothie

This four ingredient smoothie is quick to whip up and won't run you late.

Lunch: Tomato and Spinach Pasta

This dish is perfect for lunch or dinner. Make a double portion so you can have some later in the week.

Dinner: Grilled Turkey Burgers

It should never be said that you can't have a tasty and healthy burger. Fix some sweet potato fries to complete this meal.

RECIPES

Sides & Extras

Salsa

Ingredients:

- Salt
- 1 tbsp olive oil
- ½ lime
- 1 minced garlic clove
- 1/3 c coriander, chopped
- 1 jalapeno, chopped
- 1 onion, chopped
- 2 tomatoes, chopped

Instructions:

Mix everything together. Add salt to your taste. Allow refrigerating for 30 minutes.

Oven-Roasted Tomatoes

Ingredients:

salt

1 tbsp oil

4 thyme sprigs

1-pint Cherry tomatoes halved

Instructions:

The oven should be at 320. Place the tomatoes on a prepared baking sheet. Top with salt and thyme and drizzle with oil. Cook for 45 minutes.

Zucchini Chips

Ingredients:

- salt
- 1 tbsp olive oil
- 4 zucchini, sliced

Instructions:

Place the zucchini slices on a prepared baking sheet. Top with oil and salt.

Cook for 30 minutes at 320 until they brown.

Breakfast

Basil and Tomato Frittata

Ingredients:

- ½ c Italian cheese, reduced-fat
- ¼ tsp pepper
- ¼ tsp salt
- 8 egg whites
- ¼ c basil, sliced
- 2 plum tomatoes
- 1 minced garlic clove
- 2 tsp EVOO
- ¼ c onion, chopped

Instructions:

Cook the onion in a hot skillet until it has become tender. Mix the garlic until fragrant. Stir in the tomato and cook until all the liquid is absorbed. Add in the basil.

Mix the pepper, salt, and eggs. Pour into the skillet over the veggies, and top with cheese. Slide the skillet into an oven that is set to broil. Cook until the eggs are set.

Pecan, Carrot, and Banana Muffin

Ingredients:

- ¼ c pecans, chopped
- 1 tsp vanilla
- ½ c banana, mashed
- ¾ c carrot, shredded
- 1/3 c yogurt, sugar-free
- 1 egg
- 1/3 c brown sugar
- ¼ c canola oil
- ½ tsp salt
- ¼ tsp baking soda
- 1 tsp cinnamon
- 1 tsp baking powder
- 1 c whole wheat flour

Instructions:

Mix the flour, baking powder, cinnamon, baking soda, and salt together.

Mix all the other ingredients, except for the nuts. Once combine, mix into the flour mixture. Gently fold in the pecans.

Pour into a prepared 6-cup muffin tin. In should bake for 22 minutes at 375.

Homemade Granola

Ingredients:

- ½ c brown sugar
- 1 ½ tsp salt
- ¼ c maple syrup
- ¾ c honey
- 1 c oil
- 2 tsp vanilla
- ½ c dried apricots
- ½ c sultans
- ½ c dried cranberries
- ½ c coconut flakes
- 1 c cashews
- 1 c walnuts
- ½ c flaked almonds
- 1 c pecans, chopped
- ½ c pepitas
- 1 c sunflower seeds
- 8 c rolled oats

Directions:

The oven should be at 325. Mix the nuts, coconut, and oats. In a pot mix the brown sugar, vanilla, sugar, oil, honey, maple syrup and allow to boil. Let it cook for five minutes until thick. Pour the sugar mixture over the nuts and quickly stir together.

Place the mixture on baking sheets lined with foil. Cook for 10 minutes. Remove and mix up the mixture. Bake for another 10 minutes. Once it's browned, mix in the dried fruits. Once cool, seal in a bowl or bag.

Goat Cheese and Veggie Scramble

Ingredients:

- ¼ c goat cheese
- ¼ tsp pepper
- ¼ tsp salt
- 1 c egg substitute
- ½ c tomato, chopped
- 2 tsp olive oil
- ¼ c onion, chopped
- ¼ c bell pepper, chopped

Instructions:

Cook the pepper and onion until soft. Mix in the tomato and cook until liquid is absorbed. Turn down the heat and add the egg substitute, pepper, and salt. Scramble the egg until cooked through. Top with goat cheese.

Superfood Smoothie

Instructions:

- 1 banana
- 2 c spinach
- 1 c blueberries, frozen
- 1 c almond milk

Instructions:

Place everything in your blender and mix until smooth.

Lunch

Carrot and Butternut Squash Soup

- ¼ cup half-and-half, fat-free

- ¼ tsp nutmeg

- ¼ tsp pepper

- 2 14 ½ -oz can chicken broth, reduced-sodium

- ¾ cup leeks, sliced

- 2 cup carrots, sliced

- 3 cup butternut squash, diced

- 1 tbsp butter

Instructions:

Melt the butter in a large pot. Place the leek, carrot, and squash in the hot pot.
Put on the lid, and allow to cook for about eight minutes. Pour in the broth.
Allow everything to come to boil. Turn down the heat to a simmer. Place the lid
on the pot and let cook for 25 minutes. The veggies should be tender.

With an immersion blender, mix the soup to the consistency that you like.
Season with the nutmeg and the pepper. Bring everything back to a boil and stir
in the half-and-half.

Lemony Hummus

Ingredients:

- ¼ c water

- 1 tbsp EVOO

- ¼ tsp cumin

- ¼ tsp pepper

- ½ tsp salt

- 1 clove garlic, chopped

- 1 ½ tbsp tahini

- ¼ c lemon juice

- 15-oz chickpeas, drained

Directions:

Add everything except for the water and oil in a food processor. Mix until combine. Add the oil and water and continue mixing until smooth. Add extra water if you need to.

Quinoa Tabbouleh

Ingredients:

- 2 scallions, sliced
- ½ c mint, chopped
- 2/3 c parsley
- 1-pint Cherry tomatoes
- 1 large cucumber
- pepper
- ½ c EVOO
- 1 minced garlic clove
- 2 tbsp lemon juice
- ½ tsp salt
- 1 c quinoa, rinsed

Instructions:

Cook the quinoa in salted water. As the quinoa cooks, mix the garlic and lemon juice. Slowly whisk in the EVOO, and then sprinkle with pepper and salt to your taste.

Allow the quinoa to cool completely. Toss with the dressing and then mix in the remaining ingredients. Add extra pepper and salt if needed.

Curried Chicken Salad

Ingredients:

- 4 whole wheat pita rounds

- 2 c mixed greens

- 1 c green grapes

- ¼ tsp pepper

- ¼ tsp salt

- 1 tsp curry powder

- 3 tbsp mayo, reduced-fat

- ½ c Greek yogurt, nonfat

- ¼ c slivered almonds

- 1 ¼-lb chicken, shredded

Instructions:

Mix all of the ingredients except for the greens and pitas. Divide the chicken mixture into each pita. Top each with some greens.

Tomato and Spinach Pasta

Instructions:

- 3 tbsp parmesan, grated

- 1 tbsp balsamic vinegar

- ¼ tsp pepper

- 2 minced garlic cloves

- 1 c grape tomatoes

- 8 c spinach

- 2 tbsp olive oil

- 8-oz whole-wheat spaghetti

Instructions:

Cook the spaghetti the way the package says to, but without the salt. Drain.

As the pasta cooks, sauté the spinach until it wilts. Stir in the tomatoes and cook for about three minutes. Mix in the garlic.

Toss the pasta with the veggies and all the other ingredients.

Dinner

Grilled Shrimp Skewers

Ingredients:

- 9 skewers, soaked
- 1 lb cleaned shrimp
- 2 scallions, minced
- ¼ tsp pepper
- ½ tsp salt
- ¼ tsp red pepper flakes
- 1 medium lemon, zest, and juice
- 2 minced garlic cloves
- 1 ½ tbsp olive oil

Instructions:

Prepare your grill.

Mix the scallions, pepper, salt, pepper flakes, lemon juice and zest, garlic, and oil.

Place the shrimp in the mixture and coat. Allow it to marinate in the refrigerate for 30 minutes.

Place the shrimp evenly among the skewers. Get rid on any remaining marinade.

Grill them shrimp until pink and firm, around two to three minutes.

Chicken Tortilla Soup

Ingredients:

- 1 c tortilla chips

- 2 minced garlic cloves

- 1 c chicken broth, reduced-sodium

- 2 c stir-fry veggies

- 2 c chicken, shredded

- 2 ½ c water

- 1 14 ½-oz can stewed tomatoes, Mexican-style

Directions:

In a crock pot, mix the garlic, broth, veggies, chicken, water, and tomatoes.

Cook for six and a half hours on low.

Top with chips.

Rice and Beef Stuffed Peppers

Ingredients:

- 1 tbsp parsley, divided
- ½ tsp pepper
- 2 tsp salt
- 4 minced garlic cloves
- ½ c tomato sauce
- ¼ c parsley
- ½ c Parmigiano-Reggiano, shredded
- 1 ½ c rice, cooked
- 1 ½ lb ground beef
- ¼ tsp red pepper flakes
- 1 c beef broth
- ½ onion, sliced
- 2 ½ c tomato sauce
- 6 bell peppers

Instructions:

The oven should be at 375. Cut the tops off the peppers and clean out the insides. Poke a few small holes in the bottom of each.

Place 2 ½ cups tomato sauce in a casserole dish. Place in the pepper flakes, broth, and onion. Set the peppers upright in the mixture.

Mix the pepper, salt, garlic, 2 tbsp tomato sauce, ¼ c parsley, cheese, rice, and beef. Divide the mixture between the peppers. Add a tablespoon of tomato sauce on top of each and lay the pepper tops back on. Top dish with parchment paper and then tin foil. Place the dish on a baking sheet.

Cook for an hour. They should be starting to feel soft. Take off the foil and parchment and cook for an addition 25 minutes.

Jamaican Pork Tenderloin

Ingredients:

- ½ tsp pepper
- ¼ tsp salt
- 1 tbsp lemon juice
- 1 tsp lemon zest
- 1 tbsp EVOO
- 1 lb green beans
- 3 c water
- 2 tbsp Creole mustard
- ¼ c grape jelly
- 2 tsp Jerk seasoning
- ¼ c orange juice, divided
- ¾ lb pork tenderloin

Instructions:

Mix the pepper, salt, lemon juice and zest, EVOO and water. Bring everything to a boil and add in the beans.

As the beans cook, mix the mustard, jelly, jerk seasoning, and half the orange juice. Cover the tenderloin. The oven should be set and 350. Place the tenderloin in a casserole dish and pour in the rest of the orange juice. Bake for 45 minutes.

Grilled Turkey Burgers

Ingredients:

- 4 whole-wheat buns

- ½ tsp curry

- ¼ c Dijon

- 12-oz ground turkey

- 1/8 tsp pepper

- ¼ tsp garlic salt

- ¼ tsp Italian seasoning

- 2 tbsp milk, fat-free

- 2 tbsp bread crumbs

- ¼ c green onions, sliced

- ½ c carrot, shredded

Instructions:

Mix the ground turkey with the seasonings, bread crumbs, and veggies. Form the meat mixture into four patties.

Prepare your grill, and cook the patties until done.

Mix the mustard and curry powder and spread onto the buns. Add the burgers to the buns. Top with tomato and lettuce if desired.

Dessert

Blueberries and Yogurt

Ingredients:

1/3 c Greek yogurt

10 blueberries

Instructions:

Top the yogurt with the blueberries and enjoy.

Raspberry Sorbet

Ingredients:

- lemon juice
- 1 c raspberries

Instructions:

Place the ingredients in a food processor and mix until smooth. Place in an airtight container and freeze.

CPSIA information can be obtained
at www.ICGtesting.com
Printed in the USA
LVHW041915061020
668113LV00025B/1277